Salt of
the
Earth

Dedication

To my dearly beloved wife ANN – always such a positive person –
and to our grandchildren: Dan, Jonny, James, Ben, Anna, Joe and
Helen, that each may become truly positive disciples of Jesus,
who called them to be the 'salt of the earth'.

All Bible texts are from the New International Version
unless indicated otherwise
KJV = King James Version

First published in 2006
Copyright © 2006

ISBN 1-903921-33-3

Published by
Autumn House,
Alma Park, Grantham, Lincs.

Printed in Thailand

Salt of the Earth

Becoming a positive Christian

Douglas Hare

Contents

Introduction

There is a delightful story about Jesus which is not to be found in any of the gospels, but which nevertheless rings totally true.* He was walking with his disciples through a town, when they came upon a revolting sight. Lying beside the roadside was a dead dog, which an animal or vultures had ripped open, and whose exposed intestines were crawling with maggots and flies. 'Oh, Master, look! What a disgusting sight!' said one of the disciples. Jesus looked, and then replied: 'But hasn't it got lovely teeth.' Exactly! Jesus saw the good thing in an awful sight, and remarked upon it. How positive – and how sensible! Surely this should be turned into a principle for the disciple of Jesus: to look for the good points in a bad situation, to comment on the fine points in a flawed person's character, to empha-sise what is wholesome rather than what is mouldy.

This book is about being the salt of the earth, about becoming a positive person, about practising the principle just mentioned. It is so worthwhile, because it makes so much difference, both to ourselves and to those we are dealing with. Notice that the word used is *'becoming'* a positive person – not *'how to be'*, because that implies three or four easy steps to follow and then you'll arrive – and not *'being'* a positive person, because that implies that the author has got there and you haven't, and he's going to show you how to reach his level. But *'becoming'*, because it's a lifelong process, and it's mainly a spiritual one: allowing God, in Paul's fine phrase, 'to work in us that which is well-pleasing in his sight'.

So we are *becoming* positive people, which is a con-tinuing process throughout our lives of discipleship. It's simply allowing God to work in us by his Spirit, helping and enabling us, weak creatures as we are, to conform to his will. It's an ongoing process by which we should be growing more and more – very gradually for most of us, almost imperceptibly – into the likeness of Christ, who called, indeed, challenged us to *be* the salt of the earth.

* The story is credited to the famous twelfth-century Muslim poet Nizami Ganjavi.

The function of salt

The root meaning of 'disciple' is 'learner', and in the Sermon on the Mount (found in Matthew's gospel, chapters 5-7) Jesus said to his learner-disciples: 'You are the salt of the earth'. What did he mean by this, and what does it mean for us?

Salt is valued for its three main characteristics.

Freshness

First, it preserves the freshness. So we are called to preserve the freshness of the Christian faith, as deposited and received in us. We need to keep it fresh, not to get into a rut and just go through the motions, or become stale. Nor, let it be said (indeed, shouted from the roof-tops), are we to allow the essential Gospel – the absolute divinity of Christ, and the complete 'satisfaction' of his sacrifice of himself for our sins on the cross, followed by his physical resurrection on the third day – to be eroded in any way. We are preservative both of the Gospel, 'delivered once for all unto the saints', and of its freshness and relevance to us today. A good test of your own freshness is to ask yourself if you can testify about what God has been doing in your life recently. If he is working there, you'll know it!

How we need our freshness to be preserved! How easily we can become stale in our Christian discipleship, slipping into an habitual form of worship which before long becomes mere mouthing of words! And it can happen to all of us, clergymen and ministers, laity and church elders. I well recall a lay assistant minister once asking a wise bishop how he could help his minister to get out of a rut. 'Ah, yes!' replied the bishop, 'the groove that so easily becomes a grave'. And that's so true. Yet our Lord and Master tells us, 'You *are* the salt of the earth.' It's our allotted task to preserve the freshness, both of our own personal faith and the Gospel entrusted to us. The teaching of Jesus was radical and challenging. He had to break old habits of ingrained thinking (for example, the role of the Messiah), challenge fixed assumptions (for example, the Pharisees' way of keeping the Sabbath), and break down the barriers of religious practices which men put between themselves and God (for example, the sellers in the Temple).

We need to remember that God is our contemporary: He is the 'I AM' of today. He is the present tense, in fact, the present continuous!

God is alive and active, animating his people here and now. There's no way we should 'fall into a rut'. He is the God of surprises, and so we should be the people of expectancy.

We should be asking ourselves, how fresh is our vision of God, how close our relationship with him; how aware are we of his presence, both in our personal life and in our problems? All of us have difficult circumstances, but if we are Christians then we know that Christ is with us in all our troubles. And if our relationship with him is strong and secure, we shall know his strength supporting us *in* those difficult circumstances, however desperate they may be.

Easy to say, you may think, but difficult to apply. Yet

when our family experienced four hammer-blows of life within a decade – redundancy, a serious road accident, cancer, and the death of a son, which I have written about elsewhere – we could testify to the closeness of God and the support of his people in traumatic situations.

Those whom Jesus called 'salt of the earth' were very ordinary people, mostly peasants from Galilee – fishermen and bakers, smallholders and housewives – with a few professional people as well, more than likely. They probably felt like echoing their old leader Gideon who, when called by God, was so startled he blurted out, 'Who? Me?' And the clear answer was, 'Yes, you!' *You* are the salt of the earth; *you* must preserve the freshness of the Gospel; *you* must preserve the freshness of your faith; for if you don't, Jesus went on to say, people will just throw it all away!

There couldn't be a more apt warning for contemporary Christians, because the society in which we live has thrown away the Gospel as irrelevant, stale, remote and even meaningless. Today, people prefer the junk food, the quick fix, the instant answer, the throw-away platters.

Salt preserves the freshness, and so must we. It's a charge from our Master! So, how fresh is your testimony! How fresh is your application of the Gospel to today's life? How fresh is your faith? How fresh is your worship? Let's remember that Jesus called us to represent him in a fresh way to our society which so desperately needs the Salt of the Gospel.

Flavour

The second characteristic of salt is its use as a seasoning in order to bring out the true flavour of something. Its symbolic use should not be lost on those of us who call ourselves Christians, for Jesus certainly knew what he was saying – and he meant it! We are to emphasise the good qualities in people's characters, to help them reach their full potential, to see the gleaming teeth in the dead dog! More and more Churches are seeking to find people's skills or 'gifting', and to emphasises those talents and enable people to use their skills in the life of the church, either in the worship services, or in the many other worthwhile church activities.

A key issue, generally in life and specifically in Christianity, is relationships, and here again salt can, and *should*, improve the quality of relationships, and enhance the flavour. Yet Christians often fail here, although their standards (of courtesy, etc) should be better than those of non-believers. We are often amazed at how many Christians fail to say 'thank you' for a present given or a favour received. Jesus had a word about this in the Sermon on the Mount. A modern translation puts it this way: ' "If all you do is love the lovable, do you expect a bonus? Anybody can do that. If you simply say hello to those who greet you, do you expect a medal? Any run-of-the-mill sinner does that. In a word, what I'm saying is, *Grow up*. You're kingdom subjects. Now live like it. Live out your God-created identity. Live generously and graciously toward others, the way God lives toward you." ' (*The Message*, Navpress, pages 21, 22.) That really says it all: in gratitude for the grace shown by God towards us, we should be gracious towards others. Even the over-familiar Lord's Prayer has this idea built in, though we often over-look it: ' "Forgive us our trespasses [sins], as we forgive those who sin against us." ' That little word 'as' is so impor-tant. We might be more forgiving if we realised that it could mean 'to the extent that'. As forgiven sinners our-selves, should we not be more forgiving towards others?

'To enhance the flavour' should be a real concern for people called to be 'salt of the earth', and it extends far beyond actions into attitudes. I find myself being easily dismissive of some people who don't appeal to me in any way. Perhaps they appear grumpy or sour, negative or resentful. So I have to tell myself that they might be carrying heavy burdens which are weighing them down. Maybe they need a sympathetic ear or an understanding heart. If they are Christians, then they are 'salt', too, perhaps salt that has lost something of its savour. If so, their grains need to be well mixed with flavourful salt to help them to regain their saltiness!

Once I was enjoying a pub lunch with my friend Adrian Plass, the Christian author. 'So, how are things at church, Douglas?' he asked me with interest. 'Okay,' I replied, 'but there's one chap who's really a pain, frustrating my efforts, blocking our plans and generally impeding progress.' As I let off steam about this individual, Adrian interrupted me: 'So, Douglas, how are you making out with the command to "love your enemies"?'

It was a salutary rebuke, and I felt justly chastened. I put some salt on my lunch, to bring out the flavour, and took to heart the practical spiritual application, too.

A similar function of salt is to improve the ordinary, to enhance the mediocre, to enrich the drab and dreary, to enliven the dull. Some calling! But if Christ dwells within us, others should be enriched by seeing him, even in us. All who came into contact with Jesus were enriched in some way, even if it meant facing up to themselves, and the dark places in their lives. Many were healed, some transformed, and all were changed for the better by meeting him. And the most obvious way that people can meet him today is through Christians, who are called to be 'the body of Christ'.

When I first became a Christian I wanted to know who were the other Christians in the refectory at College, on the bus, or in the park. I used to think how nice and simple it would be if committed Christians could have a light bulb glowing above their heads, then we'd recognise one another immediately. And as I dwelt on that, I reflected that the intensity of our glow would reflect the degree of our commitment to Christ, the intensity of our passion for him. It wasn't long before I realised how naïve the view was. But, of course, Jesus' teaching is that we do have a light within us – *his* light – and this light is to shine out to the world around us. Immediately before Jesus said, 'You are the salt of the earth', he said, 'You are the light of the world', and later, 'I am the Light of the World'. We are the light of the world precisely because he is, and his light should shine through us. He could just as well have said, 'I am the Salt of the Earth', and we are that salt, enhancing the lives of others, simply because he is, and, amazingly, he chooses to work in us and through us.

It's a high calling, to enrich the lives of others, and to do so means being positive people. Remember that this was said to ordinary followers, not to spiritual directors or religious leaders. Because we are Christ's servants we are to add flavour to other people's lives, to bring out their good qualities, to enrich their drab existence.

One of the best ways of doing this is to use encouragement. Positive people are encouraging people! After all, life is difficult, and we all need encouragement in our efforts and struggles to get over the humps and hills. So always look for the beautiful teeth in the dead dog!

I once taught at a boys' school where we had to give 'fortnightly orders'. This meant assessing pupils in a class with A, B or C if they were in the top, middle, or bottom part of the class; but also awarding 1, 2 or 3 for effort, with 1 being the maximum effort. Once I gave a boy A-2 and another Boy C-1. The first boy complained: 'Sir, you only gave me a 2 for effort, and I got the exercise all correct; you gave Bloggs a 1, and he only got half marks – it's not fair!' I explained: 'You sailed through that exercise and did it in about ten minutes, didn't you? Bloggs took three quarters of an hour, and really sweated over it, and tried hard to work out the answers, so he gets a 1 for effort.' I'm not sure how convinced he was, but I knew he was far brainier than poor Bloggs, who was quite limited, and who needed every encouragement to tackle difficulties. His effort needed to be reflected and rewarded by encouragement.

'To enliven the drab and dreary' should apply equally to ourselves and our churches as to others. While it's true that we communicate by what we are, it is also true that we show what we are by how we appear. Anything that is drab, dull, or dreary is in need of the salt of the Kingdom. So, are our churches, and especially our church halls, reflecting the brightness and joy of Christianity? Many churches – and Christians – have little or no idea of the sort of image they present to non-Christians, nor how important it is. Our 8-year-old grandson came with me to visit his granny in hospital. Opposite was a red-brick church. 'That can't be a very good church, grandpa,' he said. 'Just look at that notice.' He pointed to a rough handwritten notice, curling at the edges, held up by a couple of drawing pins, which announced in faded tones the times and days of their services and meetings. Thus do we proclaim the good news of the Kingdom of God.

Salt should bring out the flavour, enhance the taste, so that one can say, 'This is really good!' Yet so often the impression that Christians give is of dull, boring killjoys. I once read a review in a secular paper of a movie called 'King of Kings', on the life of Christ. The critic commented that the actor playing Christ 'achieved the distinction of making Jesus seem dull'! He was, of course, rebuking him – even people of the world know that Jesus was anything but dull. Yet it's an image we often perpetuate in our churches, inside and outside the buildings, and in our worship. It is important, and salutary, to look at our image as the world does.

I once lived in a run-down seaside town, and went to a talk by a newly-appointed Development Officer. He told us that he'd asked the head of a huge chemical plant some miles away what he would recommend to improve the town and attract visitors. 'First of all,' came the reply, 'you'll need to rid yourself of the image of being a tatty seaside town.' 'I was shocked,' the Development Officer told us. He was shocked at hearing the truth from an outsider about the impression his town gave. Perhaps we Christians, the Body of Christ and the salt of the earth (that's you and me), need to hear similar truths.

In his fine book *The Jesus I Never Knew* author Philip Yancey writes, 'Two words one could never think of applying to the Jesus of the Gospels: boring and predictable. How is it, then, that the church has tamed such a character – has, in Dorothy Sayers' words, "very efficiently pared the claws of the Lion of Judah, certified him as a fitting household pet for pale curates and pious old ladies"?' The problem is nothing new. Certainly our services, our worship of Jesus, can easily become boring and predictable. How we need to be salt, to enliven the drab and dreary!

There's a story in the Old Testament of some Israelites who came to a well-situated town but found the water was brackish and the land unproductive, and told Elisha. ' "Bring me a new bowl," he said, "and put salt in it." So they brought it to him. Then he went to the spring and threw the salt into it, saying, "This is what the Lord says: 'I have healed this water. Never again will it cause death or make the land unproductive.' " And the water has remained wholesome to this day, according to the word Elisha had spoken.' (2 Kings 2:20-22.) A little salt can make all the difference!

Fidelity

If salt is valued both as a preservative and a seasoning, there is a further function which is very appropriate to our study. In ancient times, Middle Eastern countries would often use salt to ratify agreements, so that salt became a symbol of fidelity and constancy. Now there's something to ponder when you're told by your Lord and Master, 'You are the salt of the earth'! The Old Testament is all about Covenant Agreements, mainly between Israel and God. And in both Numbers and Deuteronomy we find the phrase, 'Salt of the Covenant' of your God. So by being named salt of the earth we are thereby ratifying our covenant with God, affirming our commitment to him, pledging our lives in his service.

This should lead to fidelity and constancy, both in our commitment to God and to others: to our life partner (spouse) and family, and to other Christians. Fidelity and constancy are two characteristics greatly needed in Christian circles today. Let's paraphrase them as *faithfulness* and *reliability*, and we'll see why.

Some years ago an African country was being terrorised by a particularly brutal gang who were targeting Christians. The Church Mission Society cabled the church leaders that they were praying for their safety. Back came a cable from Africa: 'Don't pray that we may be kept safe; pray that we may be kept faithful.' How wonderful! They'd got their priorities right; they knew what really mattered. They really were being 'the salt of the earth'.

A 'salted' Christian should be faithful above all else to the Master, and to others, come what may. And he or she should always be reliable, someone who won't break a promise, someone who can be depended upon. Let's make sure that we deserve the title 'salt of the earth' in all its fullness of meaning. We need to heed the warning of Jesus: 'If salt loses its savour, it is good for nothing except to be thrown out.' But we can also be encouraged by his exhortation, 'I have come that you may have *life*, and have it in full abundance.' So in our churches, in our worship services, we ourselves should show that we have *life* – in abundance.

chapter Two

Accentuate
the positive

Those who are the salt of the earth – and all Christians are called to be – must become positive people.

There was a song in my youth which went, 'Accentuate the Positive/Eliminate the negative/And don't mess with Mister In-between'! It would be a good motto for all of us, not only in our personal relations but also in our public forums: church meetings, councils, synods, whatever.

There are far too many negative Christians about, decrying the fact that things are not what they used to be (which of course they won't be when we believe in a God who is alive and active and contemporary), finding fault and blaming others, rather than finding good and encouraging others. It's all too easy to run people down, when we should be bolstering them up. Those who allow their tongues to carry them away should read the third chapter of the letter of James, until they can honestly say they have absorbed it and applied it. James, who was probably the brother of Jesus and the first bishop in Jerusalem, said, 'Everyone should be quick to listen and slow to speak' (James 1:19), and again, 'If anyone considers himself religious and yet does not keep a tight rein on his tongue, he deceives himself and his religion is worthless.' (1:26.) So, how's your religion: worthwhile or worthless?

We must apply this to ourselves as well as to others.

How quickly we bemoan our lot! Yet we should be counting our blessings, not airing our grievances. A friend of ours was a missionary in Egypt for twenty years. One day a scurrilous newspaper article about him appeared in a magazine in Cairo, and he was given seventy-two hours' notice to quit the country for ever. All his contacts, his Egyptian friends, his fellow Christians, his twenty years of service, his home, all would end. After his goodbyes, he set sail for Cyprus, and there he wrote later: 'I sat down and wrote all the blessings I could thank God for, and there were fifty-seven.' What a positive response! What a marvellous way of showing he was the salt of the earth! It sounds trite, simple and naïve, but we could all do the same: 'Count your blessings, name them one by one, and it will surprise you what the Lord has done.'

Success, the impostor

Above the players' entrance at the centre court of the All England Lawn Tennis Club at Wimbledon, which attracts tennis stars from all over the world for its great tournaments, are engraved these words from Kipling's poem 'If':

> 'If you can meet with triumph and disaster,
> And treat these two impostors just the same . . .'

A timely reminder to those who give their all to win, and become either victor or vanquished, to treat success and failure for what they are – impostors! They aren't the real values, the true standards, and yet we put a great deal of store by them.

'Success' and 'failure' bedevil churches and fellowships. We tend to count large numbers as success and dwindling attendances as failure. Yet the Bible tells us that God looks on the heart, and he is looking for devotion, for the fruit of the Spirit, for care for one another. We so easily take on board the assumptions of the world: big is better; more is marvellous! Yet it's not quantity that God is looking for; that's not how he regards 'success' or 'failure'. It's quality he wants. He'd rather have a dozen people quietly opening their hearts and lives to him than a hundred singing superficially. That's obviously polarising the problem, but a problem it is. I get little value from singing the same chorus six times; if I sing from the heart, once or twice should be enough. Then there are preachers who feel they must fill forty-five or fifty minutes, whereas their message could be relayed much more memorably in fifteen.

More is not necessarily better, and if we are to offer our worship to God it's got to be the best we can do. Similarly, the biggest church is not necessarily the most 'successful' church.

And it begs the question: how do you measure 'success' in Christian terms?

The answer in a nutshell is faithfulness.

God expects faithfulness, which means being devoted to him, putting him first in our lives, being faithful to his people, and by living out our faith. Jesus gave a clear indication of the yardstick by which we'll all be measured: ' "Not everyone who says to me, 'Lord, Lord,' will enter the kingdom of heaven, but only he who does the will of my Father who is in heaven." ' (Matthew 7:21.) Faithful obedience to God's revealed will is what counts most. Beware of 'success', and treat it for the impostor that it is.

Failure, the impostor

Equally, beware of slipping into despondency (or worse) by 'failure'. Some years ago someone publicly set up a Society for Failures, presumably feeling that they could mutually support one another, even if they were crying on one another's shoulders. He had an amazing response: headmasters, barristers, accountants, all signed up, although they had all achieved some measure of success in their professional lives. Yet they all felt themselves to be failures.

Why?

Was it because they'd failed to fill the void in their lives, because the 'God-shaped hole' in their lives was still empty?

A star footballer who played for England and was earning very handsomely admitted that he felt something was missing from his life – until he found Jesus. In one sense all of us 'children of Adam' are failures, cursed with the sin of disobedience and banished from the Garden of Paradise. A well-known hymn says, 'A second Adam to the fight and to the rescue came,' and when we are 'in Christ' our feeling of failure is banished, for we are 'right with God'.

No Christian who continues to walk with the Lord need ever feel a failure. And when we do slip and let our Lord down, he graciously picks us up and sets us on our feet again. After Peter had three times denied ever knowing Jesus, Jesus restored him and gave him a three-fold task – to care for his people.

We all let our Lord down at times, but we must then allow our faithfulness to overcome our failure. Peter, who failed his Lord at a time of great crisis, and who was eventually martyred in Rome, wrote to the Christians scattered throughout Asia: 'The God of all grace, who called you to his eternal glory in Christ, after you have suffered a little while, will himself restore you and make you strong, firm and steadfast. To him be the power for ever and ever.' (1 Peter 5:10.) Amen to that!

Hidden agenda

'Success' and 'failure' hardly appear in the New Testament, yet they are often the hidden agenda in many a church or fellowship, or for many a minister or pastor. Of course we get excited when more people attend our worship, and it is encouraging that they are coming under the sound of the Gospel, and hearing the Word of God. But the Word has to take its root in the heart and be nurtured, and any programme for church growth must be concerned with depth as much as width.

Nominal Christianity has bedevilled the Church since its foundation (see Ananias and Sapphira in Acts 5:1-11), and regular sound teaching is one way to overcome it. During the troubles in East Africa mentioned earlier, church attendance was decimated. Once the Christians were targeted for persecution, a church where normally a hundred worshipped shrank to ten. Yet the leaders rightly insisted that the church was stronger! For those ten were totally committed, and were prepared to put their lives on the line for their Lord and Master.

The phenomenal success world-wide of the Alpha course is easily explained: it simply teaches basic Christian truth in a relaxed and pleasant environment, avoiding 'churchy' language as far as possible. It is a nurture course *par excellence*, and people are responding because they feel a need to know their faith – or even to know what they are rejecting. Praise be! (We've used the word 'success' automatically in describing Alpha, almost without realising it; but we believe it is right, for it is something that God has greatly blessed and used.)

Once, after attending a performance at the Shakespeare Memorial Theatre in Stratford-on-Avon, we walked round the back of the theatre past the stage door. A lad appeared, thrust a programme and pen at me and said, 'Can I have your autograph, please?' I laughed and replied, 'You don't want my autograph: I'm a nobody.' 'That's all right,' he said. 'I like nobodies.' What a charming reply, I thought.

Yet that's what God says, too: 'I like nobodies!'

In God's eyes no one is a failure. He loves us, passionately and compassionately, and all he asks for is our obedience in love.

On the human level, Jesus was the biggest failure of all: a radical teacher and holistic healer, preaching peace and reconciliation, he ended his short life strung up as a criminal, to be mocked and jeered at by the crowds. And you think you're a failure? In God's eyes, Jesus was acting in loving obedience to his heavenly Father, and that's what matters most.

So let's not take on board the world's ideas of triumph and disaster, of success and failure. We need to keep an eternal perspective, and to see these things through God's eyes. Our own perspective will then change, and we'll find that God is approving us provided we keep faith in him, and ever seek to act in loving obedience to his will.

chapter Three

Becoming a positive person

Basic human needs

One Monday morning an angry young man burst into the church room and demanded that I tell him there and then why he should not end his life. 'I've not got a friend in the world; my girlfriend's kicked me out of her home. I've no money, and won't get any for ten days. I've no idea where my parents are, and they don't care about me anyway. I've no work, and nothing to live for. So, tell me, why shouldn't I just kill myself and end it all?'

I did a rapid mental appraisal in three seconds flat.

The first thing was to calm him down; the second was to get practical help; the third was to keep him talking, and not let him go away on his own.

I managed to get a message to the church secretary next door to contact a Christian social worker, who I knew was willing to take individuals in need into her own home, to see if she could help out. Then I faced the young man.

I was encouraged by the fact that he had wanted to see a minister first and that he wanted real answers to his very pressing questions. I was equally aware that it was totally inappropriate to say, 'Don't worry, God loves you anyway.' He didn't want pious platitudes but practical action. In an inspired moment, the words of Jesus came to me when he was confronted by an equally demanding destitute.

'What do you want me to do for you?' (Said in the positive tone of, 'I'll do all I can,' not the negative, 'I can't do anything.')

'I don't know,' he replied, rather nonplussed at my suggestion. Then he suddenly became angry again. 'I've nothing and no one to live for, nothing and nobody.'

'Let's sit down and have a chat,' I suggested.

So we did, and I gently asked a few questions about himself and his life. But first I asked his name, because your name gives you a personal identity, which helps to give meaning and significance to your life.

As we chatted and he told me a bit about himself, he gradually calmed down and talked more rationally.

Soon the message came back that the Christian lady would take him (temporarily) into her own home. So I offered to take him to a private home where he'd be given some food, shelter, and a bed for a few nights. It was an offer he gratefully accepted.

This true story illustrates that there are certain basic needs that we have in life. It is well known that *physically* we need four: food, water, air and warmth. Deprived of any one of these over a period of time, we'll eventually die. Given those four basic physical needs, we can survive – like most animals.

But we are more than animals.

We are complex human beings who have four other basic needs, and it was the deprivation of these which led that young man to contemplate suicide. These four needs – which can't easily be classified as 'emotional', or 'rational', or 'spiritual', because they are a bit of each – are as follows:

* to belong;
* to be loved;

* to be secure;
* to have a purpose in life.

The reason that the young man who burst into my Monday morning wanted to do away with himself was that all four of these *human* needs had been denied him. He didn't belong (he had no family); he was no longer loved by a 'significant other' (his girl had just kicked him out); he had no security (no home or money); and he had no purpose in life (no work).

It's important to recognise these needs, for to be deprived of any one of them can seriously mar a person's well-being. In a society that makes the pursuit of money its aim, it is well to remember that many who make their millions find deep unhappiness. For while money may supply security in abundance, it can't buy love, or even belonging, and any purpose in life may soon evaporate.

As a corollary, this emphasises the importance of a good home life, and why a cohesive family is so important for a stable society. For the home should be the place where we feel we belong. It's always sad to read of someone who has 'no fixed abode' (though, of course, that tag could be applied to Jesus; Matthew 8:20). The home should be the place where we know that we are loved, accepted for who and what we are. It should be a place where we feel secure – indeed, the phrase 'feel at home' implies security, warmth, ease, and lack of stress. And the home is the place where our characters are being formed, and where we can explore our interests in life, thus giving a purpose to our living. So the home could be – should be – the place where all four of these basic needs are met.

Now the Christian knows that he or she can have all four basic needs met in a strong faith, too.

He belongs to a Christian family: fellow members are

'brothers and sisters in Christ', who all pray to God as 'Our Father'. He is loved by a loving, personal God who has revealed himself in Jesus: 'Jesus loves *me*, this I know, for the Bible tells me so'. He is secure in that love because of Christ's promise of forgiveness through the Cross. And that gives him a new life with a dedicated purpose: to live for Christ, and to make him known, as the great commission tells us (Matthew 28:19). We'll look at all four of these basic needs in the sections that follow.

a) *To belong*

The National Census of England and Wales conducted around the turn of the Millennium asked people voluntarily to give their religious affiliation. Surprisingly, over 70% declared themselves as Christians, despite the fact that only 10% of the population attend church services. Now this significant statistic begs big questions: what do those *60%* believe in? What do they understand by 'Christian'? Do they ever worship the God they profess to believe in? In what ways do their beliefs affect their behaviour, lifestyle, priorities in life?

Yet it bears out what many ministers know. There's a great gulf between 'believing' and 'belonging'.

Time and time and time again I have visited people to prepare for the baptism of their child, to talk about wedding preparations, or to arrange a funeral, and they all say the same: 'We are believers, even though we don't go to church'; 'We are Christians at heart. We may not come to your services, but we do say our prayers.'

This is obviously a problem the church has got to face up to, and to do something about pretty quickly. For while the Christian faith still has a hold on a good many people, the institutional church obviously puts them off.

A good deal of urgent research is needed to understand why this is so. I've been in church services where there's little or no warmth of welcome, and the service proceeds along lines only the regulars can follow. Someone entering a church for a service for the first time can easily feel alienated by the unexplained ritual or liturgy or proceedings. I am aware that many come with their own agendas, with what they want and expect; if they don't find it they leave, and give up on the church, but perhaps not on their faith. Some find church services too 'happy-clappy'. Others find them too 'weary-dreary'. But those leading worship should always be aware that at every service there may be someone in the church for the first time, who needs to feel at home, rather than wish they were *at* home.

'The church is not a place you go to – it's a community to which you belong.' These wise words, whose origin I can't discover, emphasise the well-known, yet oft-forgotten truth that the church is not a building, but people. And if the church is people, then it must function through relationships. Sadly, the history of the church down the ages has highlighted those times when relationships were bad, and individuals hived off in a huff to form a congregation of those whose beliefs were similar to their own. (Only recently I met a man who stated that he was the Archbishop of the 'Anglican Independent Church'.)

The French philosopher Rene Descartes, after some days of intense concentration, uttered his famous words: 'I think, therefore I am.'

It's about time the church coined a similar sentence: 'I believe, therefore I belong.'

If you believe in the God and Father of our Lord Jesus Christ, you will want to worship him: worship is a necessary part of your belief. And although people say that they can worship God in a flower-filled garden or a sweet-smelling meadow, true worship is best expressed together, in fellowship one with another. Only then will you feel that you *belong*. At one of the services in the Anglican Church the congregation says aloud: 'We are the Body of Christ', that is, we *belong* to one another; we *belong* together because Christ is our Head.

So, 'being the church' is all about belonging to a new community, not just a 'friendly society' for mutual support, but a radically new group with different, loftier, standards and values. This community is bonded together by mutual love for Christ and a heartfelt desire to worship him. This fellowship bond is firmly secured by the adhesive of love. When Jesus called his followers 'friends' rather than 'servants', he still gave them a command, repeated three times: 'Love one another.' (John 15:12-17.) In the same chapter he commands them 'abide in my love'.

It's often very difficult to love our fellow Christian, whether he or she is tetchy or timid, contentious or complacent, and at times our co-believers can be most exasperating! How on earth (literally) are we to 'love' them? Well, in the same way as Jesus does; and so he urges us 'Abide in my love'. This will enable us to love others, even when we find it difficult to like them.

For 'love' is different from 'liking'. Love wants the best for other people, and seeks to please them. It doesn't matter whether you like them or not; you can still try to please them and desire the best for them. And this is important, most important. For Jesus gave it as the test of true discipleship, the litmus paper which will reveal the extent of our commitment to him: ' "By this all men [people] will *know* that you are my disciples, if you love one another." ' (John 13:34-35.) If those of us who call ourselves 'Christians' really took that seriously, the world would soon sit up and take notice.

For the truth is that we do belong to one another. Sociologists have identified three areas of 'belonging', like three concentric circles, each larger than the one before.

With self in the centre, the immediate and most intimate grouping is the *family*. This is where relationships are strongest (or should be), and is why supporting and preserving family life is so important. In some African countries it is the family life – usually the extended family, where even distant cousins are called 'brother' or 'sister' – that often instils an almost innate sense of duty and belonging. I've known bright young men turn down opportunities for higher education because they feel it is more important for them to work in order to pay the school fees of a younger brother or sister. Their sense of family is so strong.

The second grouping to which the individual belongs is the *tribe* or *clan*. This again is strongest in Africa, and a major cause of wars (both ancient and modern) there. Similarly, T. E. Lawrence admitted that his dream of a united Arab nation was wrecked by tribal divisions, jealousies, rivalries and the like. The tribe is a powerful factor in giving the individual a sense of identity, of belonging.

But this factor has disappeared in the Western World; we no longer think or group ourselves in 'tribes' or 'clans' (apart from a number of Scottish and Irish clans). So instead we've invented our own larger groups, bigger than our family, to which we can claim to belong. For some it's Old Boys'/Girls' groupings – reunions with classmates, Sports Clubs, Founders' Days, etc. For others it's a professional grouping, where the link is the common professional concern. For yet others, it is a local interest group – the gardening club, the amateur operatic society, or perhaps old-time dancing. Whatever it is, the significant thing is to belong to a grouping larger than the family, a group which has a focus of unity, whether it be an educational institution, a professional body, or a specialist interest.

The third grouping is the *Nation*. Our cultural heritage, our social 'mores', our national characteristics, even our quirky habits, are the things that identify us as a group, and give us a sense of the larger group identity. We cheer for our national team at the Olympics, or at a particular sporting contest, and take pride when our team wins. We are proud to be English or Welsh, to be American or Australian. Our country has a strong claim on our allegiance; so it is with pride that we can claim to 'belong' to our country, and our country acknowledges our belonging to it by issuing us with a birth certificate and a passport. It is the wide social grouping of national allegiance.

It is the same in our spiritual life: we need the three groupings to give us a sense of belonging. There's a clear example of this in the Old Testament. After the great victory of capturing the city of Jericho, Joshua sent a task force to capture the small adjacent hilltop town of Ai. They were defeated, and Joshua had to ask for God's forgiveness. God showed him that there was 'sin in the camp', and that the sin had to be rooted out. To do this, Joshua had the whole nation march past him (Joshua 7:16-18). From the nation, he extracted one clan, who then marched past him. From the clan, he took one (extended) family, who marched past him. From this family he extracted one individual, who confessed his sin. The individual is first part of the family, then of a clan or tribal group, and thirdly of a nation. And it's important to know and to feel that we are a significant part of each grouping.

Similarly, in the New Testament Jesus called twelve disciples, 'that they might be with him and that he might send them out to preach and to have authority to drive out demons' (Mark 3:14, 15). This was his core group, to be taught and trained, to be tried and tested. In the cell group, relationships are all important as the group members interact with one another over a period of time. The disciples squabbled, and often had to be rebuked by their Lord and Master (see Mark 9:33-37). Then there was the wider group of followers, the seventy or so who were commissioned to precede Jesus and to preach the Gospel, and who 'returned with joy' at the success of their mission (Luke 10:1, 17). There was also a much larger gathering of many thousands who followed Jesus (Luke 12:1), and whom on two occasions he fed – once 4,000, another, 5,000 men – and these would undoubtedly have included the twelve men of the core group, and the seventy of the larger group.

In church life today this pattern is also relevant, and the individual Christian needs to be aware of belonging to a three-fold pattern of groupings.

First there is the *cell*, which is anything from three to twenty people, with twelve being the optimum (as Jesus knew). This may be a prayer fellowship, a Bible study group, or a home group. Again, in this grouping, relationships are very important; we should feel comfortable and secure in our 'cell' (once we've got to know one another), so that we can freely share our doubts and difficulties, our hopes and fears, in confidentiality and in confident assurance, and so that we can pray for one another in our different or difficult circumstances. The cell group is – should be – an important part of a Christian's life.

The intermediate grouping is the *congregation*. Research by the Bible Society shows that this may number anything from 25 to 175. Fewer than 25 is really just a large cell; over 175 and growth stops. Note that Jesus' original 70+ had grown to 120 after the Resurrection (Acts 1:15). The optimum is about 100; and it is reckoned that one leader (pastor/minister/vicar) can effectively pastor no more than 100; above that, and another worker is needed.

In the congregation, the sense of belonging is found in the fellowship. We meet together to worship God, and that is our common purpose. In the Anglican Church, for instance, the bidding at the start of morning or evening worship is: 'We have come together in the name of Christ to offer our praise and thanksgiving, to hear and receive God's holy Word, to pray for the needs of the world, and to seek the forgiveness of our sins, that by the power of the Holy Spirit we may give ourselves to the service of God.'[1] Thus at the very outset of worship together, the purpose of the meeting is affirmed.

Our belonging together is important as a congregation. We are too many to make close relationships with everyone, though relationships are still important. (It is reckoned that the average person can make no more than sixty relationships.) But fellowship can and should be nurtured and encouraged, so that people feel they 'belong'. A test of that feeling is that they are missed if they don't turn up for a couple of times to worship with the congregation; so a phone call or a visit is required.

The third grouping is the *celebration*. This is a gathering of 180 or more Christians to celebrate together, to join with fellow-believers in worshipping God in a large assembly — the bigger, the better.

Here the *event* is all-important, and the focus of attention: it is therefore vital that this is of a high standard.

In a large gathering there is no place for any real relationships. It is the event that binds us together, as we worship and praise God, and hear his word to us.

In England, the largest celebration is 'Spring Harvest', an annual Eastertide festival held in a number of centres, which attracts thousands of people of every denomination annually. Significantly, one has to book about nine months beforehand to be sure of getting a place. These celebrations are almost always interdenominational and are the better for it, for we celebrate simply as Christians, not as Methodists, Adventists or Anglicans.

Other celebrations take place in cathedrals ('Pentecost Praise'); at camp meetings (often held in holiday camp settings); or in the open air (Greenbelt); wherever a large assembly of people can gather. One gathering that is highly popular takes place in a concert hall, emulating 'Last Night at the Proms' in a Christian setting, and called 'Prom Praise'. These are usually very stimulating and inspiring occasions, sending us back to our churches and fellowships with a song in our heart and a spring in our step.

For far too many years, church and fellowship members have been content to be only a part of a congregation. As a result, their spiritual growth is stunted, as they are deprived of the value of 'feeding on the Word' in a cell, learning to pray together and to care for one another. They are deprived, too, of the warmth and enhancement of a celebration, so their Christian life gets into a rut of routine. They see it as their Christian 'duty' to go to church, to take part in a service, rather than to celebrate together in fellowship with other believers. But the Christian family is bigger than the local congregation, important as that is.

Every Christian needs to be a part of a three-fold grouping: the *cell* and the *celebration*, as well as the *congregation*.

In the cell, we make close Christian relationships which support one another through prayer and practical pastoral care, and encourage one another in discipleship; in the celebration we find ourselves rejoicing in being a partnership with God's people from other denominations, from different traditions, from other areas, from different countries. Both will help us so much more to feel that we belong to God's people, his Church.

b) *To be loved*

At the end of a Remembrance Day service which I'd taken I was saying 'Goodbye' to the members of the congregation as they left the church. A middle-aged lady whom I'd never seen before grasped my hand and suddenly burst into tears. Embarrassed, she choked, 'I'm sorry – it was my Dad; he was killed in the war.'

I softly murmured some words of condolence, but she suddenly blurted out, 'Can I talk to you for a moment?'

She obviously needed to, so we went back into the church and sat down together in a pew. She'd composed herself by then, and looking straight at me said, 'It wasn't really true; it wasn't my Dad I was crying for; it was myself. I just happened to be in this town today. I've come from Liverpool to see my sister, and I just felt I wanted to go to church. I'm so desperately unhappy. You see, both our parents are dead, my sister's my only relation, and she's just told me that she doesn't want any more to do with me; she's quite self-sufficient with her husband and two children and never wants to see me again' (and here the crying started again). 'I don't know why – I've never done anything wrong. I lead a decent life. I life with a chap, but we don't love each other; it's just convenient that way. So there's no one, no one at all, who loves me. If I were to die tomorrow, it wouldn't make any difference to anybody else, and no one would come to my funeral. That's why I'm feeling so upset.'

Another mega-sized pastoral problem to be dealt with in three minutes (I had another service to take).

As I shot an arrow prayer to Heaven, I took her hand in both of mine (the warmth of touch is expressive and important). 'I want to tell you,' I began, 'that you are very important to God. You're his child, and he really loves you. *He* cares about you, and I believe he's guided you here today. He knows about you, and he wants to wrap his loving arms around you. Didn't we pray together in this service "Our Father"? He's a Father who loves and cares about his children. And everyone here prayed that prayer, and that means we are brothers and sisters, through our Christian faith. Now, I'd like to pray for you. Is that all right? (She nodded.) So tell me your name.' 'Jeannie.' 'All right, Jeannie, I'm going to pray that you may know God's peace in your heart, and his love in your life.'

Still clasping her hand, I prayed a simple prayer that she might experience for herself the love of God in her life. When I'd finished, the tears had dried up, and there was a slight smile on her lips. She suddenly gave me a peck on my cheek, and I realised she felt that someone had bothered with her, and it had given her a sense of significance. As we went back to the church door together I gave her a booklet from the bookstall which affirmed God's love for her, and which would show her clearly how to find God's special love for herself.

How important it is to know that 'Somebody loves me'! It's why the family unit is so significant, why divorce or separation, both for adults and for children, is so hurtful and diminishing. We sometimes hear of 'tug-of-love' cases where children are torn between two warring parents, or of children fostered in one family being claimed back by the birth parents. But the criterion must surely be not who will provide for the child, but who will truly *love* the child, giving him or her time, attention, reading a book to him, listening to her, taking an interest in all the child's doings – so much more important than just providing something to eat and a place to sleep. A child needs to experience the outgoing, overflowing love of a parent – ideally both parents – and to be secure in that love. Sadly, it is often the child who is starved of love who in later life finds it difficult to love others.

To be loved is a basic human need. To know that I mean something to someone else indicates that I am worth something to one other person at least in a world which often seems harsh and impersonal. 'All you need is Love' is (still, I believe) a popular song, because it expresses a universal feeling, a need to be loved. God's plan for humanity is that this love should be experienced within the family. The parents have a mutual love for each other, and that overflowing love is shared with their children, who know from the beginning what it means to be loved.

But 'love' is a mushy word, with different layers of meaning, and needs defining. Basically, the person who loves wants to please the beloved, to do the best for him or her (which is why you can still love a child whom you need to rebuke). Love seeks the best for loved ones, tries to say/do/give things which will delight them and bring them happiness. It springs from the heart, and so must be heart*felt*. Which is why we need to grow in love, to develop and continue to grow all the time. Otherwise we become stunted, and our love atrophies.

One of the best ways of growing in love is to read

(together, perhaps, with your beloved) chapter 13 of 1 Corinthians. Read this daily for a month. Memorise it if you can. After two weeks put the name 'Jesus' in place of 'Love'; after three weeks put your own name in place of 'Love' or 'it' (in verses 4-7). It's a challenge, but it should help to make you more loving, and more lovable.

Yet 'love' can be easy to say but hard to show. Songs from musical plays often reflect this: 'Don't talk of love – show me!' sings the girl in the musical, *My Fair Lady*. A song of my youth had a line, 'With all your faults, I love you still', which reflects real love, and that is exactly what God is saying to you and to me. In *Oklahoma!* (my favourite musical) a girl who is being courted by a two-timing sales-man sings to him: 'With me, it's all or nothing;/is it all or nothing with you?/It can't be in-between; it can't be now and then/no half-and-half romance will do.'

I don't consider it irreverent to remark that that is exact-ly what Jesus is saying to you and to me. It's all or nothing with him! His words are worth pondering: ' "Love the Lord your God with *all* your heart and with *all* your soul and with *all* your mind. This is the first and greatest command-ment." ' (Matthew 22:37, 38, emphases mine.) No half-and-half commitment will do. It's *all* of you I want, he says, for your own good, and so that you can experience my overwhelming love for you in all its fullness.

We use this wonderful word 'love' far too loosely. Obviously, 'I love burger and chips' just means 'like very much', but it really misuses 'love'. Sometimes it is used for the sexual act ('make love'), but this should be the expres-sion of a deep personal love, not a substitute for it.

The Greeks wisely separated the different strands of 'love' into three:

The first they called *'Eros'*, which stands for physical love pure and simple (the word 'erotic' comes from it).

Then there's *'Philos'*, which is like brotherly love, a deep-seated, strong affection, with a highly developed trust and confidence in one another.

The highest form of love was called *'Agape'*, rarely used in classical Greek, but used throughout the New Testament. It is defined as 'the highest and noblest form of love, which sees something infinitely precious in the beloved.' (*The Illustrated Bible Dictionary*, IVP, 1980.) What a wonderful definition! And it is used to describe God's love for you and for me. God loves us with an 'agape' love; we are infinitely precious to him. Now there's something to sing 'Hallelujah' about, to shout from the rooftops!

The dear lady who burst into tears at our Remembrance Day service felt that nobody loved her: she didn't mean anything to anyone. ('If I died tomorrow, no one would come to my funeral.') Well, God would be there, and I tried to reassure her that in God's sight she was infinitely precious to him. We all need to be loved, and to know for certain that someone cares about us. That is the found-ational message of Christianity: God loves me, even me!

c) *To be secure*

If one is aware of belonging to a caring group, such as a family, and of being loved by someone, for example, a parent, then this usually provides a firm foundation of security. But suppose the parents split up: disharmony creeps in, and the security is shattered. Mum has to go out to work, to become the bread-winner, and as a result is often not at home when the child returns from school. At weekends the child leaves the familiar family home and spends Saturday and Sunday with Dad, who perhaps has acquired a girlfriend and who finds it difficult to contrive ways to interest and entertain his offspring. So the child grows up with a basic insecurity.

Many people are insecure, but most keep it hidden. Some compensate by being over-confident, which shows itself in arrogance, even aggression. Others exhibit nervousness and a general lack of self-confidence. Yet others spend their time trying to convince others (and themselves) what good people they are. A deep-seated fear of appearing incompetent, or a failure, is the underlying agenda for many.

The best antidote to this is encouragement. It means affirming someone's strong points, and not picking on their faults. To be actively encouraging others is a mark of a positive person. Paul's companion Barnabas was known as 'Son of Encouragement' (Acts 4:36) because of his positive attitude. He it was who introduced the newly-converted Saul to the apostles in Jerusalem, and persuaded them that his conversion was genuine and that he really had met with Christ – at a time when Saul must have felt very insecure indeed.

One of the ways to strengthen people's security is to help them to feel accepted. Conversely, rejection is a large contributory factor in engendering insecurity. Some months ago I watched a television programme which chronicled the doings of a Christian support charity in South London. A youngster of 18 or so turned up at the hostel seeking help; he'd been adopted as a child, but now his adoptive parents wanted his room, and had thrown him out. The hostel gave him food and shelter for six weeks, but then had to turn him out because he didn't fit into community life. My heart went out to this young man, and a tear rolled down his cheek (and mine) when he was told he couldn't stay. What a terrible feeling of rejection he must have had to bear: rejected by his natural parents, rejected by his adoptive parents, now rejected by a Christian group. With nowhere to go, no home, no work, no purpose in living, no security, no 'fixed abode', what a sense of total insecurity he must have felt. The documentary didn't follow him: it just showed him wandering off on his own. I felt not only sad but angry. At the very least the Christian community should have arranged to place him in a loving, caring and supportive environment; maybe they had, but the programme didn't even imply it.

It is most important for a child – and a youngster – to feel secure, and the same is true for a new Christian. In many ways, he or she is thrown into a new culture, with unfamiliar attitudes and different priorities. Once you invite Christ to take over the driving seat of your life you may well find yourself in unfamiliar territory, which could tend towards insecurity. The eminent philosopher, Sir Isaiah Berlin once stressed the 'radical difference' between people who believe that God made them for a purpose and wanted them to spend eternity with him, and those who did not: 'The reasons for action, the moral codes, the political beliefs, the tastes, the personal relationships of the former will deeply and systematically differ from those of the latter.' (*Concepts and Categories*, Oxford University Press.) He perceived that it makes a huge difference to a person's attitude, actions, priorities and 'reasons for behaviour' when he or she puts their trust in Almighty God. So it's important for new believers to find that security in Christ, to whom their lives have now been entrusted.

But this has an effect on our worship. Too often in my life I have had to ask myself, 'Would I be happy to ask a new Christian or a seeker to our church worship?' and frequently the answer has been 'No!' Our ritual, our jargon, our mode of worship — all are totally unfamiliar to the new-comers. Even minor matters — when to stand up or sit down, where to find the right place in the service book — can be off-putting, and induce a feeling of not being 'one of them', and so apart, and thus, insecure. Even the most self-assured person can feel insecure in an unfamiliar setting. I remember reading an article by a brash journalist who'd been invited to a Church christening. His piece was humorously entitled, 'I knelt down and prayed that God wouldn't zap me!' He described with complete amazement the unfamiliar (to him) ritual, and obviously felt a complete outsider — and thus insecure in a situation which he couldn't handle.

It's important for churches and fellowships to address this situation sensitively. We've probably all heard stories of people who'd come into a church for the first time to worship, only to be told that they were sitting in the churchwarden's pew, or that they couldn't take communion, or that they'd broken some convention — and they'd never returned. I love the story (told by Rebecca Manley Pippert in her excellent book *Out of the Salt-shaker*, IVP) of the dishevelled and unkempt student who came into a church just before a service and could find no seat, so walked up to the top of the centre aisle and sat down on the floor. A pinstripe-suited churchwarden with polished shoes thereupon strode up the aisle, while the congregation held their breath, expecting confrontation. But they were amazed when the churchwarden stopped by the student — and sat down alongside him. Well done, that man! By so doing, he made the young man feel accepted and not a stranger.

Churches and fellowships need to be aware of different ways to help all the members of their congregation feel secure in their faith. Ways of engendering fellowship, such as sharing meals together, family day picnics, or projects such as a working party in the church or grounds, a cleaning day in the building, can do a great deal to foster the sense of being part of the 'Body of Christ'.

Equally, members need to know their faith. While sermons are useful for encouragement, instruction and exhortation, they are not the only way to 'teach the faith'. They need to be supplemented by, for example, small group Bible study, where the members meet in a home and study a passage or book of the Bible for an hour each week. These groups need to be places where members feel comfortable and secure, confident that the group will not laugh at their ignorance nor betray a confidence. These of course are the cells, mentioned earlier, to which Christians need to belong. Becoming an accepted part of a cell leads to confidence and security.

Most importantly, Christians should be assured of finding their total security in the Lord Jesus Christ. Throughout the Scriptures, and particularly in the words of Jesus, we find positive promises on which the Christian can rely. Here are just a few of the words of encouragement which Jesus gave to his followers:

'Come to me, all you who are weary and burdened, and I will give you rest.'

'My peace I give to you.'

'I call you my friend.'

'You are in me, and I in you. Abide I me, and I will abide in you.'

'I am with you always, even to the end of the world.'

'Even the very hairs of your head are numbered.'

'I am the Way (for you), the Truth (for you), and Life (for you).'

If the Christian ponders these wonderful words, he or

she should never feel insecure!

d) *To have a purpose in life*

The fourth basic need for an individual, both in personal life and in Christian life, is to have a purpose. We've all heard of 'drifters', those sad people who drift through life without any drive or motivation, without purpose or meaning. In the old days in our Western culture the woman found meaning and purpose in running a home, and in nurturing and rearing children, while the man found purpose in his work.

But nowadays, life for both has to be more than that.

There's the old saying of the labourer who stated: 'I dig a ditch, to earn the money, to buy the food, to give me the strength, to dig a ditch.'

Is there no more to life than that? Of course there is, and most people find outside interests to enrich their lives. It may be in music, joining a choir or an orchestra; in sport, supporting a major team or playing for a minor one; in hobbies or crafts, or even in religion.

For 'religion' (a word I'm not very fond of, and which hardly appears in the New Testament) can give meaning and purpose to life. If we believe in a Creator God who created us for a purpose, this should be the basis of our lives, the drive behind our living. St Augustine expressed it beautifully thus: 'Thou hast made us for Thyself, and our hearts are restless until they find their rest in thee.' That should give us a purpose for living!

To find God's will for our lives is both motivating and exciting. I can remember now the deep satisfaction I felt when I knew that God was calling me to become a teacher: it was a true vocation. But when I came into a deeper relationship with God during college, it dawned on me that he wanted me as a teacher *abroad*. I'd not reckoned on this, and I didn't really want to be a missionary teacher at all. My sense of purpose wasn't helped when my father said, 'They say that if someone's no good at anything, he either joins the army or becomes a missionary.' I'm not at all sure who 'they' are who say this tripe, but obviously 'they' do not appreciate the physical courage of the soldier, nor the moral courage necessary to go abroad with the Gospel message. Better to take Isaiah's words to heart: 'How beautiful on the mountains are the feet of those who bring good news, who proclaim peace, who bring good tidings, who proclaim salvation.' (Isaiah 52:7.)

So I went, and spent ten fulfilling years in Africa as a missionary teacher, and trainer of teachers. Times were sometimes tough and difficult, but I knew I was in the place of God's appointing, where he wanted me to be, and that gave contentment. Paul wrote: 'I have learned to be content whatever the circumstances' (Philippians 4:11) – and he wrote *that* when he was in prison! He was content because he was in God's will and purpose for him, and that gave him an inner peace.

Notice that 'being content' doesn't necessarily mean having favourable circumstances. Paul was content, though in his writings he tells us: 'Five times I received from the Jews the forty lashes minus one. Three times I was beaten with rods, once I was stoned, three times I was shipwrecked, I spent a night and a day in the open sea, I have been constantly on the move. I have been in danger from rivers, in danger from bandits, in danger from my own countrymen, in danger from Gentiles; in danger in the city, in danger in the country, in danger at sea; and in danger from false brothers. I have laboured and toiled and have often gone without sleep; I have known hunger and thirst and have gone without food; I have been cold and naked. Besides everything else, I face the daily pressure of my concern for all the churches.' (2 Corinthians 11:24-28.) And people still say that Christianity is a prop, a crutch, a soft option!

We all know that there is more to life than working for the weekly pay packet or monthly salary. And the rich who live and 'party' in an endless pursuit of pleasure will find that, in time, it does nothing to satisfy inner longings. If, as the French mathematician Blaise Pascal exclaims: 'We all have a God-shaped hole at the centre of our lives', then we find the purpose for our lives when we allow God our Creator to come into our lives and fill up the hole with himself.

There are countless stories of people today whose lives have been turned around once they have allowed Christ to fill the aching void. Former terrorists who now devote their lives to helping people; ordinary people whose lives are transformed by Christ's power and direction; celebrities who've found fame and fortune but not contentment in their star status, yet have found it in Christ. One such is Margaret Court, triple Wimbledon champion in the 60s. She used to go along to church regularly, and sit through the rituals each time. Then she thought, 'There *must* be more to Christianity than this,' and began to explore ways to deepen her burgeoning faith. She had a powerful experience of God's Holy Spirit, and is now a dedicated pastor and evangelist.

We don't all have a high-profile calling; maybe our purpose in living is fairly humdrum, we may be confined to a wheelchair. We may be a hard-working mother with demanding kids, a care assistant looking after old people, or a road sweeper. A good friend of mine is a cheerful

Christian dustman. But as George Herbert wrote: 'Who sweeps a room, as for thy laws, makes that and th'action fine.' It's from a poem (also a hymn) whose first verse goes 'Teach me, my God and King, in all things Thee to see, And what I do in any thing, to do it as for Thee.'

That's the secret of having a purpose in life: living for God.'

[1] *Common Worship.* Archbishop's Council 2000.

The most positive person

'Who do people say that I am?' Jesus once asked his disciples. The very place where this important question was asked was significant: the Bible names it Caesarea Philippi, a pleasant place near the foot of Mount Hermon, whose melting snows form the source of the Jordan river. But it had another name, Paneas, because there was a temple and shrine there to the Greek god Pan, where people regularly worshipped. It was a very pagan place. The disciples were quick to chip in with their answers:

'Some say John the Baptist.'

'Some say Elijah.'

'Others say Jeremiah, or one of the prophets.' (Matthew 15:13-16.)

This was the common view, that Jesus was one of the great prophets come back to life, a belief that might have stemmed from an Old Testament verse (Deuteronomy 18:18) where God said that he would raise up a prophet from among the people. But such an answer would not be forthcoming nowadays.

So how would people respond if that question were asked today? The makers of a video *So who is this Jesus?* (CTA, Bristol BS48 1PG) decided to ask a dozen people in the street who they thought Jesus was. The replies are illuminating: A man spiritually enlightened; Someone who helps people; No idea (3 times); A messenger of God; Someone special; A religious icon; A good bloke – like other good blokes; He came down to help us all; Son of God – our Saviour; Someone who did a lot of good.

So the knowledge of who Jesus really is remains vague and distant today. People see him as a cult figure, with little concern to them, or *for* them. Others with some Bible knowledge imagine that he strode through life untroubled by its difficulties, performing miracles here and healings there, ably supported by a band of devoted disciples, until, in a sudden, violent act of gross injustice, he was crucified after a mock trial, and then three days later rose from the dead, thus vindicating his claim to divinity.

For many years I thought of him as a sort of Superman, who could turn on his divine power at a touch. Then I read the story of the woman who'd had internal bleeding for twelve years, and whom no doctors could cure. When she reached out and touched Jesus in faith, the bleeding stopped and she was cured. But Jesus called out, 'Who touched me? For power has gone out of me.' (See Mark 5:25-34.) Power had gone out of him! It was then that I realised that he wasn't 'Superman' at all, and the truth of Christian teaching all down the ages dawned upon me: Jesus was fully God, and fully man, and not half-and-half of each, as I'd thought. As fully God, I worship him; as fully man, he understands me.

After asking the disciples the people's opinions of him, he asked them the question he asks everyone: 'Who do *you* say that I am?' It was then that Peter blurted out the great truth: 'You are the Christ, the Son of the Living God!' And if we acknowledge that, we must ask ourselves if we therefore submit to him as our Lord and Master.

The four brief biographies of Jesus (called 'Gospels')

which we find in the New Testament, reveal someone who experienced nearly all the hardships that could happen in one short life. Yet throughout he remained calm, balanced, and a charismatic leader of men, always puncturing pomposity and hypocrisy. One example will suffice: anyone who has been a soldier will know that the first and basic rule you learn is that you obey orders *without question*. Yet when the chief priests sent the temple guards to arrest Jesus, they came back empty-handed. 'Why didn't you bring him in?' they asked. The guards replied, 'No-one ever spoke the way this man does.' (John 7:32, 45-46.) As a former soldier, I find that quite amazing.

No Superman

He was born in a cave in a hillside. As a toddler he was taken to Egypt as a refugee from the tyranny in his own country. Returning later, he grew up in Nazareth, learning his father's trade as a carpenter. In his late twenties he left home, was baptised by his cousin John, and at once went into retreat in the wilderness, where he suffered starvation and temptation. Returning, he began to teach and preach about God's Kingdom, which he said had arrived. But the religious leaders were so incensed at this upstart that they tried to silence him; thus he became a 'wanted' man. Even the people in his own home town tried to kill him. He had no home to call his own, no job, no security. His own family virtually disowned him, believing him to be mad. His closest followers exasperated him in their failure to grasp his message. When a good friend died, he wept. A close friend denied he ever knew him, and another betrayed him. He was arrested for a crime he never committed, and died the most cruel and barbarous death ever devised by man. He went through it all, and at the end, when he needed them most, most of his friends forsook him and fled. He knew what it was like to receive the hard knocks of life, if anyone did. Yet he preached, 'I have come that you may have life, and have it in all its fullness.'

I regard Jesus as the most positive person who ever lived, and one who was never afraid to 'buck the trend'. Not only did he upset the religious leaders by healing people on the Sabbath, but in a male-dominated society he showed compassionate concern for women and children. One example: at a well in Samaria he asked a Samaritan woman for a drink of water. Yet the Scriptures tell us that 'Jews have no dealings with Samaritans'. The woman was so surprised that she answered: 'You are a Jew, and I am a Samaritan woman. How can you ask me for a drink?'

Jesus was breaking down social, racial and religious barriers all at once.

Eventually she called her Samaritan friends to meet him, while his Jewish disciples returned from their shopping expedition. The Samaritans were so impressed with Jesus that they urged him to stay with them; so he stayed there a couple of days. And because of his words, many more became believers. They said to the woman: 'We no longer believe just because of what you said; now we've heard for ourselves, and we know that this man really is the Saviour of the world.' (See John 4:41-42.) So meeting with Jesus himself brought these alienated people into a living faith.

The Lord of the Second Chance

So there was Jesus, despite his weariness and thirst (no 'superman' he!), flouting convention and bringing those despised Samaritans into God's Kingdom. And the same is true for other outcasts – sufferers of leprosy, for example. These poor people had to ring hand-bells as they went about outside, shouting 'Unclean'. What a humiliating way to have to live! Yet Jesus went out of his way to touch them, to heal them, to affirm them as human beings. Again, he sought out the hated tax-collectors. Those people were regarded as traitors because they collected taxes for the detested Romans. Because they had contact with Gentiles, *and* lived off the extortionate margin they added to the rate of tax, they were regarded as ceremonially unclean, and so were excluded from the synagogue. But Jesus drew them into the Kingdom of God. Zacchaeus of Jericho was one of the best-known examples (Luke 19:1-10), while Matthew of Capernaum was chosen to be one of the twelve apostles. Soon after his decisive response to the call of Christ, he gave a party for his fellow-tax-gatherers to meet Jesus. When rebuked by the legalistic Pharisees for consorting with such outcasts, Jesus replied, 'It's not the healthy who need a doctor, but the sick.' (Matthew 9:9-13.) Jesus refused to go along with the totally negative attitude of others.

The gospels abound also with stories of his positive actions: turning water into wine at a wedding feast ('You've kept the best till last'), feeding the hungry multitudes, calming a deranged 'maniac'. When confronted by the madman of Gadara, who was kept chained hand and foot, the first thing Jesus did *was to ask him his name.* Thus he recognised him as a person, as a human being with an identity, an individual personality. It is our names which identify us in society.

He also helped people to adopt positive attitudes for themselves. When a man in the crowd called out, ' "Teacher, tell my brother to divide the inheritance with me," ' he responded, ' "I'm not going to judge between you; but don't be greedy; there's more to life than possessions." '

(Luke 12:13-15, *my paraphrase.*) When confronted by the woman taken in adultery, whom the law said should be stoned to death, he invited those without any sin to cast the first stone. As they all crept away ('beginning with the eldest') he just said to her, 'Go, and sin no more.' How important it is to cultivate and adopt a positive attitude to people, however awkward, and to situations, however difficult.

'Ungrace'

Yet how often is our attitude to others more than just negative, even wounding and hurtful at times? Do we show disapproval with glaring looks at the baby in church crying during a service? Do we smirk at the unkempt young man with long matted hair, wearing an old T-shirt and jeans, wandering into 'our' church? Do we stare with pursed lips at the stranger who unwittingly sits in the churchwarden's pew or the deacon's seat? These are random examples, but they can put people off Christianity pretty quickly. It should remind us that negative attitudes are 'out' for the committed Christian.

But it's a lesson we find hard to learn. Even a cursory reading of the gospels shows us that *love* should be the hallmark of the Christian disciple: 'My commandment is this: love one another as I have loved you' (John 13:34); 'By this shall all men know that you are my disciples, if you have love one for another' (verse 35); 'If you love me, keep my commandments' (14:15) – all the words of Jesus to his disciples, then and now. And yet Christians, more than most, it seems, find it very difficult to accept, let alone love, those whose ideas or doctrines are different from their own sometimes narrow or blinkered particular views.

Philip Yancey, the journalist and author, in his excellent

and challenging book *What's so Amazing about Grace?* (Zondervan) tells of the '*un*grace' which he found in so many churches. He cites an instance when he wrote an article, 'The Riddle of Bill Clinton's Faith', for which he'd done much research and personal interviews, and concluded, 'I found it almost impossible to understand the Clintons apart from their religious faith.' But his article unleashed a torrent of hostile criticism from Christians of all denominations. He received mail-bags full of angry letters and writes, 'Less than ten per cent of the letters had positive things to say, and the vicious tone of the personal attack caught me off guard.' He concludes, 'In twenty-five years of journalism I have received my share of mixed reviews. Even so, as I read through stacks of vituperative letters I got a strong sense of why the world does not automatically associate the word 'grace' with evangelical Christians.' (Pages 227-8.)

We all probably need to repent of our 'ungrace', and ask God to forgive us and to grant us a positive attitude to those with whom we disagree. 'Love one another, as I have loved you.'

'The divine original in everyone'

Yet how do we love as Jesus loved? Christianity tells us to hate the sin, but love the sinner. To separate the two is not easy, but we are called to do so, and Jesus gave us many examples in his dealings with people. 'To love a person,' said the Christian author Dostoevsky, 'means to see him as God intends him to be.' Remember the disgusting dog with the gleaming teeth! The German pastor Helmut Thielcke spelt it out: 'Jesus [had] the power to love harlots, bullies, and ruffians. . . . He was able to do this only because he saw through the filth and crust of degeneration, because his eye caught the divine original which is hidden in every way – in *every man*. . . . First and foremost he gives us new eyes. . . .

'When Jesus loved a guilt-laden person and helped him, he saw in him an erring child of God. He saw in him a human being whom his Father loved and grieved over because he was going wrong. He saw him as God originally designed and meant him to be, and therefore he saw through the surface layer of grime and dirt to the real man underneath. Jesus did not *identify* the person with his sin, but rather saw in this sin something alien, something that did not really belong to him, something that merely chained and mastered him and from which he would free him and bring him back to his real self. Jesus was able to love men because he loved them through the layer of mud.' (Quoted in Yancey: *What's so amazing about Grace?* page 175.) The positive person sees through the layer of mud with new eyes; the negative person sees only the mud.

Even at the end of his short life, when in the anguish and agony of the crucifixion, Jesus speaks positively. Seeing his broken and bewildered mother weeping (who, as we recall, was told at his birth, ' "He will be great and will be called the Son of the Most High . . . he will reign over the house of Jacob forever" ' (Luke 1:32-33; 2:35), he commits her care and well-being to his beloved friend John: ' "Dear woman, here is your son", and to the disciple, "Here is your mother." ' (John 19:26-27.) To be concerned so much with another's well-being when in one's own death-throes is the action of the most positive person.

c h a p t e r

A Church in need of salt

The too-taut tension

In order to make beautiful music, the strings on any stringed instrument, from harp to guitar, from violin to double-bass, must be in the right tension.

A slack string will produce no music, while a string that's too tight will soon snap.

The instrument has to be 'in tension', but that tension must be right.

The Christian is someone who has to live 'in tension' too, and it's important that he's neither too slack nor too taut. We're in tension because we are 'in the world' yet not 'of the world' – we live as fellow human beings in our society, and are deeply affected (even infected) with its standards and values, however slack and relative; yet we are also citizens of the Kingdom of God, where the standards and values are sharp and absolute. For example, the Church has to uphold absolute moral standards, yet show compassion to those who fail to keep them (hence its dilemma over remarrying divorcees in church, and in its attitude to homosexuals and transvestites). There's a taut tension there all right, and often it snaps!

Again, our faith is compounded by paradoxes, which need to be held together in creative tension: Jesus is both fully God and fully man; we receive new life through his death, God is immortal, yet Jesus dies; the perfectly good man is crucified as a common criminal; the Creator of the whole universe becomes a vulnerable babe. There's quite a tension holding these near-contradictory truths together, and the easy temptation is to abandon one or the other. But hold fast to them both we must, for we are charged to maintain the faith in all its freshness and not to debilitate it for our own convenience.

The Church, too, lives in a number of tensions. One of these is its style of worship. Is it to be a gathering for the faithful, an in-house event for those who come week by week, and thus where the newcomer feels an outsider? Or is it to be geared totally towards the outsider, and thus sacrifice its church language and ritual to be completely 'user-friendly' to those it is seeking to draw in? Perhaps there could be a compromise between the two, or two services, one for each group? The fastest growing church in the world (and second largest), Willow Creek in Florida, took the unusual step of holding a worship service for its members on a mid-week evening, while offering Sunday morning 'presentations' for the unchurched – a 'service' without ritual, liturgy, collection, church language, notices, robes, hymns, Bible reading, sermon, prayers, yet which presented the Gospel through music, drama, dance and song – all of a high standard – together with a brief talk on a relevant topic or current issue from a Christian view-point. And the non-Christians, the unchurched, flocked to it, so that now there has to be a second 'presentation' on the Saturday evening as well.

Far too many churches – especially their congregations – have failed to realise, yet alone resolve, the tension between providing a service for their own members and reaching out to the unchurched. The attitude to the enquiring unbeliever is 'welcome; come and join us *but on our terms*', that is, with all our ritual and language and churchy paraphernalia which is probably incomprehensible to the uninitiated. I know of one minister who wanted to introduce a family service just once a month (that is, twelve times out of fifty-two in a year!), but was opposed by the regular (mainly elderly) worshippers on the grounds that 'it would spoil *our* service'! Perhaps they'd never heard William Temple's famous dictum that 'the Church is the only Society that exists solely for the benefit of its non-members'; or they'd forgotten Jesus' great commission to his followers: 'Go into all the world and preach the Gospel to every creature.' Once a church becomes a cosy club for its own members, self-protective and totally inward-looking, it is doomed, and no longer deserves the title, 'church'. The tension is lost, the string has snapped, and no sound comes forth.

So, what is a Church meant to be? For a start, the church is people, not a building. A wise man once said: 'Church is not a place you go to, but a community to which you belong.' A church community is a gathering of very different people from very different backgrounds and up-bringing, who are united in their desire to follow Jesus. They gather together to worship him, to learn more about him, to seek to become better disciples. They are people who have to earn a living in the world, yet are citizens of the Kingdom of God. And that produces a taut tension. I once attended a prayer breakfast in a town where I was giving a course on Friday evening and all day Saturday. The host said: 'I wonder if Bob's coming.' Then he turned to me and said, 'Bob lives on a knife-edge; he's a salesman, and in his business you're only as good as last month's returns.' Bob didn't make it, but it gave me an insight into the tension in which some people have to live all the time.

There's also the ethical tension: is the business cutting corners, manipulating people, fiddling figures? Many an employee must have asked him/herself: how do the ethics of the business I'm involved with square with the ethics I find in the New Testament? And if there's a conflict, what do I do about it? For many businesses, the aim is solely to make money rather than to give a good service at a fair price. I was once briefly associated with a very large travel organisation, and was given a copy of its staff handbook. I was surprised (perhaps naïvely) to find that the stated aim of the company first and foremost was 'to make a profit'. So everything was seen in monetary terms. I should have thought that a better aim might have been 'to give such a good quality service, in courtesy, efficiency, and provision of facilities on time, that customers will continue to use us, and will commend us to others.' That, of course, would lead to profit-making, and also help to motivate staff the more!

'There will always be the Church and the World,' wrote the poet T. S. Eliot, 'and the Spirit of God fluttering between the two.' How true! And that makes for tension. The Spirit is not only, or always, in the Church, but also in the world; and the Christian has to live in both. The easy temptation is to separate the two into different compartments of our lives, and not allow them to overlap. I once heard of two men who worked in the same department of a bank; it was twelve years before they realised that they were each treasurer of different churches in their city, that they were both Christians. Jesus teaches us to bring worldly wisdom into church affairs (Luke 14:27-33), and to bring spiritual wisdom into our business affairs (Luke 6:35-45). It can create a tight tension; but then the *right* tension produces the best music.

So it's important to recognise that the note we sound as a church fellowship should be pleasing to God's ear. We need to get the tension right: not too taut, not hidebound by a rigid liturgy and predictable inflexibility, leaving no room for eager expectation or excited anticipation for our worship service, nor so slack that the informality obscures due reverence and proper standards. A musician is constantly adjusting the tension of a stringed instrument to get it just right. The leader of a church or fellowship needs to be aware that the tension may need constant adjustment to produce the best balance.

Adapt and change

For the Church to remain credible in current society it will have to adapt and change. Not, I hasten to add, its Gospel: this is truth unchanged, unchanging; truth that is valid for all societies for all time. But its relationship to society will have to change, for it's no good thinking that the old ways were good enough in the past, and they'll continue to be so in the present.

The times of our services, the length and structure of our worship, the style of our singing (use of organ/robed choir/guitar/singing group), all need to be considered.

If we stick with the past, society will view us as a relic, irrelevant for today. There are no easy answers, but the questions must be faced.

Always remember the tension: too slack – an over-relaxed and informal style of worship without any reverence or dignity; too taut – a rigid adherence to an outmoded pattern without any resonance with modern society. Both will produce only a pathetic sound.

The whole concept of getting people into churches (buildings) needs to be examined. Shouldn't the church be going out to the people? In the gospels and Acts it was the Christians moving out, visiting towns and villages, that spread the Gospel. There are similar movements today: the March of a Thousand Men, in different areas or countries, sharing the Good News in pubs and sleeping in church halls; and On the Move, an initiative providing a free lunch in a city centre with a Gospel message and the opportunity for personal prayer. These are commendable activities, and a valid way of taking the Christian message to where people are, rather than waiting for them to come to us. It is, of course, a method pioneered by our Master himself, when he sent out seventy-two disciples to all the villages and towns to which he himself would come; we can read their briefing (Luke 10:1-16; Matthew 10:5-42), and their report: 'The seventy-two returned with joy and said, "Lord, even the demons submit to us in your name." ' (Luke 10:17.) Perhaps a similar witness today would result in people turning to the Lord.

There are even those who would say that we should get out of church buildings altogether, and close them down or sell them. The Church, they claim, should not be bound by walls. I sometimes lead worship ('take a service') and preach in a village church. Last time I went it was a family service; yet there were only eight people present, and no children or youngsters at all. In the porch was a typed notice: 'We are in desperate need of an embroidered Bible marker, cost £25.' And I wondered if that reflected the priorities of that small yet faithful congregation. Does not 'a *desperate* need' show a blinkered and parochial view, a concern for the adornment of the church building rather than for the enlargement of the church with people?

Further, would it not be better for those eight people to meet in a home each week for fellowship and prayer, Bible reading, meditation and singing, instead of channelling their energies into trying to raise funds for the upkeep of an old building and the provision of Bible markers? Meeting informally in a home makes it easier to ask a friend or neighbour to join us to worship God and to learn more about the Christian faith.

The Christian West needs to look at China. In 1958 the government had closed all visible churches; Mao's wife told foreign visitors, 'Christianity is dead and buried.' In the 1970s a visiting Christian delegation reported, 'There is not a single Christian left in China.' Today, the Chinese church numbers tens of millions, greater than it has ever been; and all without a church building. (Quoted in *Back to Jerusalem*, by Paul Hattaway, Piquant Press, 2003.)

It was a wise and experienced man of the world who once said: 'The death knell of any organisation is sounded when people say, "We've always done it this way."' Adaptation and change are a necessary part of life, and the Church will be left behind if it fails to take account of this. So I welcome modern translations of the Bible, for example, which seek to bring out the meaning more clearly. Some new paraphrases, such as *The Message* come across quite startlingly, but then the Gospel message *should* jolt us! And I'm saddened by the organisations which seem to be committed solely to preserving the past, such as the Prayer Book Society, that rightly loves the enduring poetic prose of the *Book of Common Prayer*, yet forgets that in its day (1662) it was contemporary language. Clinging to the past will make matters more irrelevant to the present.

But I don't want to sound too cavalier about this.

Change for change's sake just will not do. I'm quite fond of quoting a line from Shakespeare's *King Lear*: 'Striving to better, oft we mar what's well.' Change needs to be seen to be better, and to win the consent of those it will affect the most before it's initiated.

Sometimes change has to be drastic. There are churches which have uprooted their fixed wooden pews in order to provide more flexible and comfortable seating. The bonus, of course, is that the chairs can be moved, so that different areas of space and groups of seating can be formed. This in turn means that church buildings can be used for many functions to enhance community life at different times. It is pretty wasteful to have a 'plant' — a church building — which is used for only one day in seven. Why not adapt it so that it can be an amenity for the community for six days a week as well? A live and positive church might host a Mums & Toddlers' group, and/or serve lunches for the elderly once a week. There are all sorts of opportunities for churches to adopt, and once they seek to serve the community the community might be more inclined to come to their services.

One church group I know has abandoned its inflexible building, preferring to hire the local school hall for its Sunday morning worship. Why not? Other church groups I've heard of bought a pub, renamed it 'The Carpenter's Arms', and hold meetings and services there for a different kind of congregation. Innovative change like this may well cause people to sit up and take notice. If God is calling us to be the salt of the earth, we mustn't become stale, but add spice to our witness to a needy society.

Yet Christian ministers and congregational leaders need to recognise that 'change' needs careful handling. It mustn't be imposed upon an unsuspecting congregation, who may resent the disruption of the established order and familiar practice. It is essential to inform, even educate, the congregation/fellowship first, and as far as possible win them over. Presumably the change is taking place to fulfil a purpose, to pursue a vision. So explain the purpose, share the vision with those most affected by the change, and seek to gain their consent. If they see the reason, and catch the vision, they'll agree, and the change should go smoothly. I once pleaded with the leader of a church at which I was an assistant minister to 'educate the people', before he introduced radical change. 'We educate them by doing it,' he retorted, and promptly lost a sizeable following as people voted with their feet. Change needs careful management, patient listening, bold decisiveness and careful explanation to become acceptable to a congregation or fellowship.

We also need to be aware of the underlying philosophy of our age. Whereas in the past the criterion for a concept or belief was, 'Is it true?' in today's postmodern society – wherein so much is relative, including the truth – the question becomes, 'Does it work?' Thus an explanation of a creed or tenet of faith backed by Bible verses will cut little ice today. 'That may be true for you,' it is said, 'but it doesn't make it true for me. What I want to know is "Does it work?"' So the best witness is personal testimony, and, of course, changed lives. We are back to St Francis of Assisi's dictum: 'Preach the Gospel at all times; use words only if necessary.'

I'm a great believer in the power of personal testimony, which I believe is both undervalued and under-used. Once when a student, I went to a service in a fairly staid, conservative, Protestant church. The young man leading worship suddenly said, 'It's every Christian's privilege to give his testimony' – and proceeded to give his. So it should be, but it is rare for Christians to be taught or encouraged to share their experiences of the God of all Grace, either spoken or in writing. Yet it can have a powerful effect. My 17-year-old son gave his testimony at a home meeting, and a lady in her late 30s was deeply moved. 'If it's true for that young man and means so much to him, then it can be true for me,' she thought. The next day she sought out the minister's wife, who led her to a living faith in the Lord. I was pleased to see that my grandson, together with other youngsters of the Youth Group, had to give a personal testimony before being baptised by immersion. There's nothing like a personal account of one's conversion and experience of the Lord for answering positively the unasked question, 'Does it work?' So why not include a testimony, or an interview with a believer, in your worship service, say once a month?

There's many a church that needs a pinch of salt, something to spice it up, to freshen its worship, and to enhance its taste and flavour. Certain it is that the Church must adapt and change, and while it must never conform to the standards and values of secular society, it must be able to engage with the prevailing culture. The style, content, and even the timing of our worship should – no, must – take account of 'where people are' today, for it is pretty certain that they are not in church. While about 5.5% of the population of the UK attend church, that means that possibly 94.5% do not know, love, or care about the God and Father of our Lord Jesus Christ. Yet many churches go on in the same old way, oblivious it would seem to the utter indifference of most 'outsiders'.

Nearly fifty years ago, the writer J. B. Phillips was one of the first to translate the New Testament into contemporary

English. His vigorous comment in his preface to his translation of the Acts of the Apostles is worth quoting at length. 'The reader . . . is seeing Christianity, the real thing, in action for the first time in human history. The new-born Church, as vulnerable as any human child, having neither money and influence nor power in the ordinary sense, is setting forth joyfully and courageously to win the pagan world for God through Christ. . . . Here we are seeing the Church in its first youth, valiant and unspoiled – a body of ordinary men and women joined in an unconquerable fellowship never before seen on this earth.

'Yet surely this is the Church as it was meant to be. It is vigorous and flexible, for these are the days before it ever became fat and short of breath through prosperity, or muscle-bound by over-organisation.

'These men did not make "acts of faith", they believed; they did not "say their prayers", they really prayed. They did not hold conferences on psychosomatic medicine, they simply healed the sick. But if they were uncomplicated and naïve by modern standards, we have ruefully to admit that they were open on the God-ward side in a way that is almost unknown today.'

He concludes, 'Perhaps because of their very simplicity, perhaps because of their readiness to believe, to obey, to give, to suffer, and if need be to die, the Spirit of God found what He must always be seeking – a fellowship of men and women so united in love and faith that He can work in them with the minimum of let or hindrance . . . consequently, (this) small body of ordinary people so moved the world that their enemies could say . . . "these men have turned the world upside down" (Acts 17:6).' (*The Young Church in Action*.) 'Surely this is the Church as it was meant to be' – and could be in our generation.

The need to grow in grace

'Grace' is one of the great words of the New Testament, and so it should be, for it describes God's total self-giving for mankind. Here's Paul: 'God is able to make all grace abound to you, so that in all things, at all times, having all that you need, you will abound in every good work.' (2 Corinthians 9:8.) Note the fourfold 'all', and also that good works are the *result* of God's grace, not a way of earning it.

So what *is* grace? David Watson had a mnemonic: **G**od's **R**iches **A**t **C**hrist's **E**xpense. It's a good way to remember, but it needs unpacking.

This unpacked material would include the following: Unmerited favour, undeserved mercy, unearned forgiveness and unconditional blessing. For grace is the totally unde-served blessing of a gracious God, received through faith in Christ's sacrifice on the cross. The children of grace are mercy, forgiveness and compassion. None of it is earned, and none of it is deserved. No wonder it is described as 'amazing'.

It was John Newton who wrote that wonderful hymn 'Amazing Grace', and he wrote it from personal experience. His second line 'that saved a wretch like me' rings very true. For Newton was the captain of a slave trader, ferrying cap-tured slaves from West Africa to the Indies and America. Once the ship was hit by a fearsome storm which almost threw him overboard. He cried out to God, and underwent a dramatic conversion. For a little while he continued to trade in slaves, but then left the sea to become an Anglican minister. He soon joined William Wilberforce to campaign for the abolition of slavery. He was so ashamed of his past, and so amazed at God's acceptance of him, that he wrote

'Amazing Grace' in gratitude. He would fully understand these fine words of Paul: 'You know the grace of our Lord Jesus Christ, that though he was rich, yet for your sakes he became poor, so that you through his poverty might become rich.' (2 Corinthians 8:9.) So what, I wonder, do we have to do to become 'rich in grace'?

If it is unearned, undeserved, unmerited in any way, the answer must be – nothing! A lot of Christians have great difficulty in accepting this. They feel instinctively that they must *do* something to deserve God's mercy and forgiveness and blessing. But 'nothing in my hand I bring, simply to thy cross I cling,' wrote Augustus Toplady the hymn-writer, and he was right.

When the profligate son came home to his father, having wasted all his inheritance, he said simply, 'Father, I have sinned against heaven and against you. I am no longer worthy to be called your son. . . .' What was the father's reaction? 'Bring the best robe, a jewelled ring, and let's have a party! My son was lost, and is found; was dead, and is alive again!' The son did nothing; the father did everything – all was grace (Luke 15:11-32).

Many people outside the Church, and quite a few in it, believe vaguely that scales of justice determine our eternal destiny. All our good deeds go into one pan, all our bad deeds are put into the other, and if our good deeds out-weigh our bad deeds, we go to heaven. If it's the other way round, we go to the other place. But this is contrary to all Christian teaching. If it were true, then Christ died in vain, for there'd be no need for a cross.

A truer though still imperfect picture would be that all your bad deeds go into one pan of the scales, and the cross of Christ (with your name on it) goes into the other, and the bad deeds all melt away. We are saved solely and simply through the sacrifice of Christ on the cross, and not because of anything we have done. Someone put it this way, 'There's nothing we can do to make God love us more; there's nothing we can do to make God love us less.' God's love combined with his grace is total, personal, and unconditional. Receive it!

Many Christians today need not only to grasp the concept of grace, but also to grow in it. And the first step is to realise all that God has done in order 'to save a wretch like me' – that is, to contemplate the cross. A young mother who'd recently been converted told me that she slipped into a church one morning, sat in a pew and gazed at the depiction of Christ on the cross in the stained glass window. 'I just burst into tears,' she said, 'when I realised that he'd done all that for me.' She was growing in grace.

This realisation of 'all that he's done for *me*' will lead to thanksgiving. So give thanks daily: give thanks for Jesus, give thanks for the cross. Count your blessings, and praise God for them. Paul again: 'The grace that is reaching more and more people may cause thanksgiving to overflow to the glory of God.' (2 Corinthians 4:15.) An awareness of God's grace leads to a grateful heart.

Someone may well say: 'That's all very well for you; you don't know the problems I've got. Sometimes they overwhelm me.' I sympathise, and I understand. But I'm not being unrealistic or triumphalist, nor burying my head in a sand-pile of piety. There's great truth in that fine old chorus:

'Turn your eyes upon Jesus,
Look full in his wonderful face,
And the things of earth will grow strangely dim,
In the light of his glory and grace.'

As we look to Christ and receive his love, our own problems will be seen in perspective, and will surely diminish.

And I speak from experience of hardship and pain.

Our second son was killed in a road accident at the age of 27. We grieved deeply, but were quite overwhelmed by an almost tangible awareness of the love of God, both directly in our personal grief and also as expressed through his people. So we still give thanks for Mike, and for the way in which God used him to bring new life to others. When asked how many children we have, we still say proudly, 'Three' – he's still our son. His loss pained us deeply, but he's still a blessing.

A growing awareness of God's grace will enable us to share it with others. Like love, grace is reciprocal: the more you receive, the more you give away; the more you give away, the more you receive. So the more we recognise and experience God's grace in our lives – his forgiveness, his mercy, his compassion – the more we'll be able to exercise grace towards others.

A major figure of the Old Testament was David, 'a man after God's own heart', we are told. Yet he was an adulterer, and (by proxy) a murderer. But he repented (see Psalm 51), and despite his failings he received God's grace: 'I will pour out on the house of David . . . a spirit of grace.' (Zechariah 12:10.)

A major character in the New Testament is Paul, who was used by God to spread Christianity throughout a vast area, and whose letters to churches still nurture people in the faith today. Yet he had been a rabid opponent of the followers of Jesus of Nazareth, a persecutor of Christians, who stood by in approval at the stoning to death of Stephen. He knew, deep in his heart, 'the grace of our Lord Jesus Christ'.

Sometimes church business meetings close with the saying of 'The grace' from 2 Corinthians 13:14. Too often its use can be perfunctory, and it can easily become hackneyed and superficial. May I suggest and recommend a slightly expanded version to bring out the true meaning:

'May the amazing grace of our
Lord Jesus Christ make us gracious;
And the abounding love of God make us loving;
And the abiding fellowship of the Holy Spirit
bind us together in one in him,
To his praise and glory, Amen.'

The need for assurance

If it is our privilege, as Christians, to give our personal testimonies or tell of our experience of God's grace in our lives, it is equally necessary to be certain about our beliefs, to be sure of our faith, and to *know* what we believe. Peter wrote to his flock: 'Always be prepared to give an answer to everyone who asks you to give the reason for the hope that you have.' (1 Peter 3:15.) So we are challenged by Scripture to give convincing answers if asked why we are believers in the Christian faith.

What are the certainties of our faith to which we firmly hold? We need to know our faith, not in an arrogant manner, but in humble confidence, 'with gentleness and respect' says Peter.

I would suggest that there are two extremes to avoid, two pillars to build on, and two questions to consider.

The two extremes to avoid are * blind faith and * blindness to truth.

Having blind faith will lead one to believe anything. I suspect that in this country there are more people who read their horoscopes each day than who read their Bibles every morning. And they take them seriously! Someone is born in a particular month, yet many consult and believe them. Our assurance must be built on evidence, not on blind faith.

At the same time, we are not to be blind to truth. There are many people who would call themselves 'Christian', yet who don't believe in the resurrection of Jesus from the dead. This despite the fact that countless scholars would agree with the eminent judge who declared that 'the resurrection is the best attested fact in history'.

Some years ago a very learned man wrote to a Sunday newspaper bemoaning the decline in Christianity in this country; he suggested that if the Church gave up its 'ridiculous' belief in the resurrection of Christ from the dead, people would flock into our churches once more. I am pleased to say that there was a spate of letters the following week affirming the indisputable fact of the resurrection. Being blind to truth is as unhelpful as taking things in blind faith.

But there are two pillars on which we can build our assurance of faith.

The first is objective truth, and the second is subjective experience.

Both are equally important. It is no good having one without the other.

There are plenty of people who say the creed, and mean it, but they have no experience of the living Christ in their lives. They state and believe the truths of the faith, but it plays little part in their lives; it is head knowledge, not heart knowledge.

It is when we *experience* the truths that we can be certain about them.

Equally, it is not enough to rely on experience alone. Someone can have ecstatic visions, but they must be grounded in scriptural truth, otherwise any interpretation can be put upon them; and this is the highway to heresy.

So were do we find truth?

The Christian would say, in the Word of God.

And 'Word of God' has two meanings:

First it is Jesus himself (John 1:1, 14) who states, 'I am the truth' (John 14:6).

Second, it is the Bible, which is a record of God's Word to mankind.

Let us continue to look at the resurrection: how do we know it is true?

First, consider the story of Thomas. He wasn't a 'doubter'; he was *sure* that Jesus had not risen from the dead. When told that he had, Thomas made conditions: 'Unless I . . . put my finger in the nail marks in his hands . . . I will not believe! When the risen Christ came to him, showed him his hands, and said, 'OK, Thomas, put your fingers here,' Thomas could only kneel down and worship: 'My Lord and my God!' (John 20:24-31.)

I would also point to 1 Corinthians 15:3-8 where Paul lists all the people who saw the risen Christ. So there's the objective truth; but allied with it is the subjective experience: that the risen Christ lives within my heart, and is a vital part of my life. The famous Swiss theologian Dr Karl Barth wrote fourteen volumes of Christian dogmatics. When he visited America on a lecture tour a brash reporter asked him: 'Dr Barth, could you express your beliefs in just a couple of sentences?' The learned doctor smiled, and said simply: 'Jesus loves me, this I know, for the Bible tells me so.' It may sound simplistic, even naïve, but in reality it's all there. It contains assurance ('I know'), built on the twin pillars of personal experience ('Jesus love *me*') and truth ('the Bible tells me').

Another example. In John's gospel chapter 9 there's a quite lengthy account of Jesus' dealings with a man born blind. Jesus heals him and restores his sight, but the religious leaders cannot bring themselves to acknowledge it. They claim that the man who has been healed cannot be the man who was born blind, but another who happens to look like him (vv. 8, 9, 18). They send for his parents to verify that it is their son who had been born blind, and to explain how it is that he can now see (vv. 20-23). The religious leaders tell the healed man that the one who has cured him is a sinner (v. 24). The man expostulates: I don't know whether he's a sinner; but 'one thing I do know. I was blind but now I see!' (v. 25.) When they insult him (v. 28), he gives a testimony to Jesus (vv. 30-33). As a result, they throw him out of the synagogue (v. 34). But Jesus goes and finds him, and asks him to believe in (trust) the Son of Man. The man says, 'Lord, I believe', and worships Jesus. He's had a personal experience of the touch of Jesus upon his life, as well as knowing something about him.

So to the two questions. First, do you *know, for a fact*, that your sins are forgiven – and why? The first part of the question demands a yes/no answer: 'I hope so' will not do! The imagery that Bunyan uses in *The Pilgrim's Progress* is very vivid. When Christian stands facing the cross, the burden of sin on his back falls off, and rolls downhill into a 'sepulchre', where it disappears forever. Our sins *are* forgiven because of the cross, and for no other reason – certainly not because of anything that we ourselves have done. So let us thank God daily for his forgiveness through Christ's atoning sacrifice on the cross.

The second question demands a straight answer, too. Do you *know* that there is life after death? You only have to read the gospels carefully to be aware of the great emphasis Jesus put on the fact of judgement. One example will suffice: 'Not everyone who says to me, "Lord, Lord," will enter the kingdom of heaven, but only he who does the will of my Father who is in heaven.' (Matthew 7:21.) So there is a judgement, for sure. But there is also an assurance. Jesus was crucified between two criminals. One railed at him, cursing God; the other trusted: 'Jesus,' he requested, 'remember me when you come into your kingdom', and Jesus replied, promising him a place in paradise. (See Luke 23:42, 43.) Now that promise was given only to the thief who repented and trusted, not to the other one. Our response to Jesus determines our eternal destiny. Paul affirms this: 'We believe that Jesus died and rose again and so we believe that God will bring with Jesus those who have fallen asleep in him. . . . And so we will be with the Lord for ever.' (1 Thessalonians 4:14, 17.) John affirms in his gospel probably the best-known words in the whole of Scripture: 'For God so loved the world that he gave his one and only Son, that whoever believes in him shall not perish but have eternal life.' (John 3:16.) But the promise is only to those who believe (trust) in him.

If you want to be sure of your forgiveness and your eternal destiny, soak yourself in God's Word, and claim his promises. Paul wrote to some uncertain Christians: 'I *know whom* I have believed' (2 Timothy 1:12) – '*whom*', not '*what*'! Be assured! Know – and trust – him whom you have believed.

A truly salted church needs to be full of assured people.

chapter Six

Positive discipleship

1 The Church

a) *People*

'The Church', say some people, 'is full of hypocrites.' What do they mean, and why do they say it?

It would seem to mean that those who go to church should lead near-perfect lives, and never do anything remotely wrong. Certainly the behaviour of many church-goers leaves much to be desired, and for this we should repent. But being remade in the image of God is a lifelong process. As the car sticker puts it: 'God hasn't finished with me yet.' But the 'world' seems to think that the church *should* be full of saintly 'good-goodies', and certainly, we should be growing in the grace of Christ, and asking him to control our tempers, to manage our thought-lives, to increase our patience.

But in reality the church is not full of hypocrites; quite the opposite. The church is full of people who are sinners, most of whom are prepared to admit it! Some churches I know put a sign outside: *This Church Welcomes Sinners*, or even *For Sinners Only*. The first thing we do in a church service is to admit our sinfulness, and to seek Christ's promised forgiveness. Rather than being hypocrites who pretend that we are good, we are sinners who admit that we are bad!

Yet our lives have to match our faith: our behaviour must reflect our beliefs. We don't become 'good' overnight: God has to work in us, and as far as some of us are concerned, it's very hard work for him! He has to break down our prejudices, our ingrained habits, our cultural lifestyles. He has to re-order our priorities and teach us that we are now citizens of the Kingdom of Heaven with a higher allegiance, as well as citizens of the kingdom of Earth.

And there are many who *don't* learn, and some who *won't* learn. It has been said that the biggest obstacle to the spread of Christianity is – some Christians! Sad, but probably true. Jesus knew the importance of his followers having a truly Christian lifestyle. *The Message*, a paraphrase of the New Testament in modern language, puts the ending of Jesus' Sermon on the Mount like this: ' "These words I speak to you are not incidental additions to your life, homeowner improvements to your standard of living. They are *foundational words* [my italics], words to build a life on." ' That's why we need to 'read, mark, learn, and inwardly digest' the words of Scripture.

One of the more amazing things about our God is that he chooses to use ordinary people like you and me to spread the Gospel of his grace; and despite our flounderings and failings he goes on using us. How privileged we are! The church, as we need to keep on reminding ourselves, is not a place we go to, but a community to which we belong. And a community consists of ordinary people like you and me, who are simply seeking to live for Jesus Christ, to reflect him in their lives, however feebly. This is why we need to grow in grace, to grow in our knowledge and application of the Scriptures, to grow in our discipleship. Growth implies nurture, which means both discipline and exercise. And unless we grow, we atrophy and dry up. So we need to ensure that our spiritual life is developed properly by a balanced diet of worship, prayer, Bible reading, service and fellowship. And this demands self-discipline.

It is often forgotten that self-discipline (or self-control) is one of the fruits of the Spirit mentioned by Paul (Galatians 5:22, 23). Christians need to remember this: self-control is a gift of the Spirit, and where the Spirit of the Lord is, there is freedom to exercise self-control – a freedom that comes from the Spirit of God, not from the striving of man.

Yet many Christians have failed to exercise self-discipline, and by acting in unchristian ways we have put countless people off the faith. The story is told of an eminent man who was retiring from a demanding job. He'd been very active and busy in his work, so he was asked what he would do in retirement. He replied: 'I've been looking for a place to run, to take in all those people who have been hurt by the church; the trouble is, I can't find anywhere nearly big enough.' It may be apocryphal, but there's a ring of truth about it.

The Church consists of people who walk to a different drumbeat. Their priorities are those of the Kingdom of God, not the kingdoms of this world. Their values are the absolutes of God, not the relatives of man. They know they have experienced the love of God in their lives; they know their sins are forgiven solely by God's grace; they know they are privileged to be called the children of God, and to be the disciples of Jesus. It's a high calling: let's make sure that we live up to it!

b) *Worship and fellowship*

If we believe in God at all, we will want to express that belief by worshipping him. Worship is our response to our awareness of God's love for us – personally. Because 'I know my sin's forgiven, I'm on my way to heaven', I respond by offering my worship to the God who loved me enough to die for me, to redeem me, to forgive me. So how should I express that worship?

The answer is – in almost as many ways as there are people. Some prefer a ritual or liturgy from which there is no departure at all. Others prefer a more relaxed, less structured, style of worship. Still others would want nothing planned at all, so that they are led entirely by the Spirit. Yet in all the diverse styles of worship there are two vital elements that must be present:

> * the worship must come from the heart,
> * and should be in company with others.

The scriptural meaning of the word 'worship', both in Greek and Hebrew, is 'service', originally signifying the labour of slaves or hired servants. My Bible dictionary states: 'In order to offer this "worship" to God, his servants must prostrate themselves . . . and thus manifest reverential fear and adoring awe and wonder.' (*Illustrated Bible Dictionary,* IVP.)

This 'adoring awe and wonder' is usually expressed in praise and prayer.

So our praise (normally involving music) and our prayers are expressions of love and gratitude to God, real acts of inward, spiritual worship. Thus it can be expressed in a wide variety of ways; but the essential point is that it must spring from the heart. Remember what Jesus said was the first commandment? 'The first commandment is this: you shall love the Lord your God with all your heart, with all your soul, with all your mind, and with all your strength.' Most readers emphasise the four different nouns; I would emphasise the four-fold 'all'. No half-hearted worship will do; it has to involve us totally: mentally (mind), physically (strength), spiritually (soul), and emotionally (heart) – and each one has to be 100%. It's all of *us*, for *all* of him! So our worship should be a total experience, involving us completely, as we express our wholehearted devotion to God for his wholehearted grace and love for each one of us. Whether this is formal or informal may well depend upon our upbringing, our culture, or our inclination. But whatever, let's be sure it springs from the heart.

The second characteristic of true worship is togetherness. God's church is made up of individual people, but true heartfelt worship is when the local church – the body of Christ – shares together in expressing its love for God. Love develops and spreads as it is used (like a smile), and mutual love for God expressed in worship becomes fellowship.

The most common act of worship is the meeting together of Christians ('the church') once a week. It is important that this gathering engenders fellowship. In fact, we affirm in our service: 'We are the body of Christ', which is biblically true (1 Corinthians 12:27), while the sharing of 'the Peace' – which I believe originally came from the Church of South India – is an awareness of our oneness in Christ, and thus of our fellowship together.

Does this mean that one cannot be a lone Christian, a believer who worships God in his or her own way and privacy? One can be, and there have been hermits and spiritual recluses all through recorded history. But it is better by far for us to identify with other Christians in the locality, and thus add to and strengthen the body of Christ in the place where God has put us. Let us worship God together, then, and let this worship be heartfelt. Whether we find this best in ritual and liturgy (which for some is too casual, for others true freedom), or in informality and free expression, the important point is that it is reverence from the heart. We should always be expectant when we come to worship, expecting to meet with God, expecting that he will meet with us, so that we can learn something from him. Expectant, too, as we meet with others, to learn from them, so that as the body of Christ we can begin to approach Paul's ideal: 'From him [Christ] the whole body, joined and held together by every supporting ligament, grows and builds itself up in love, as each part does its work.' (Ephesians 4:16.)

Notice that it's not passive: 'each part *does* its work'. And what is that work? It is building up the body of Christ in love. This means mutual acceptance, quite possibly exercising forgiveness, certainly sharing fellowship, and it's often costly.

What do you do when you fall out with someone in the church? Certainly try to meet together, to pray together, then to share a meal together. Perhaps you will read aloud together Paul's first letter to the Corinthians chapter 12, verses 12-27; and maybe go on to the famous 'hymn to love' in chapter 13.

The Palestinian pastor Elias Chacour tells how just after his ordination he was asked to be the pastor of a village church. He arrived full of eagerness but was greeted – by the man meant to welcome him – with the words: 'Go away! Get out of here! We don't want you here. Do you understand? Go away!' Poor Chacour was emotionally poleaxed by such a 'welcome', but had the grace and courage to say, 'Let's pray together.' The other man was taken off guard as Elias prayed, 'O God, draw us together as Christian brothers. Help us to work out our differences.' (Chacour, *Blood Brothers*, Kingsway.)

One of the most challenging of all Jesus' statements to his followers must be:

'By this all men [people] will know that you are my disciples, if you love one another.' (John 13:35.)

Sadly, the history of the Christian Church all down the ages has far too often been characterised by bitter disputes with members publicly exhibiting a great lack of love. Yet many people have been won for Christ by his servants showing true love, by going the extra mile, by compassionate caring. And if we really show his *agape* love for one another ('the highest and noblest form of love, which sees something infinitely precious in the beloved'), then undoubtedly the world will sit up and take notice.

There needs also to be more sincerity in our worship. Our hearts need to be involved, not just our minds. And we need to reach out to one another, to share Christ's love together. Sometimes we feel that drastic action is required to jolt people out of their complacency, out of their sub-Christian attitudes and example. Pastor Chacour tells how he laboured for eighteen months in a village, but those who came to church were filled with bitterness and hatred for one another. They went through the motions of worship, but their hearts were not involved, and they'd emerge from a church service still bitter enemies. He knew that shock treatment was needed. So at the end of the service on Palm Sunday, just as the people expected him to give a blessing, he marched down the church, closed the great doors, and securely padlocked them. Returning to the front, he faced the congregation.

'Sitting in this building does not make you Christians,' he

began. 'You argue, you hate each other, you gossip and spread malicious lies. Surely your religion is false. If you can't love your brother that you see, how can you say you love God, who is invisible? You have allowed the body of Christ to be disgraced.' The reaction was silent shock and suppressed anger. He went on, 'For many months I have tried to unite you. I've failed, because I'm only a man. But there is someone else who can bring you together in true unity. His name is Jesus Christ. He is the one who gives you power to forgive. So now I will be quiet and allow him to give you that power. If you *will not* forgive, we will stay locked in here. You can kill each other, and I'll provide your funerals *gratis*.'

The tension was palpable. The silence hung, and lasted. Three minutes, five, eight, ten: still that hard, thick, heavy silence endured. After fifteen minutes a Palestinian police-man got to his feet. 'I am sorry,' he spoke falteringly. 'I am the worst of all. I've hated my brothers, sometimes so much I have wanted to kill them. More than any of you, I need forgiveness.' Elias called him forward, and he walked up to the priest; they embraced, and greeted each other with the kiss of peace.

'Of course I forgive you,' said Chacour. 'Now, go and greet your brothers.'

So the floodgates were opened. At once the church was awash with tears of repentance, and tears of joy at recon-ciliation, of acceptance, of forgiveness. A second church service, lasting nearly an hour, took place – a liturgy of love and reconciliation. (Chacour, *Blood Brothers*, pages 170-2.)

This surely is the church as it is meant to be: a commu-nity of love and reconciliation. And I sometimes wonder what the reaction would be if Chacour's brave deed were carried out in our churches. I have known occasions when a sermon on forgiveness resulted in someone getting up out of a pew, and going across to another person to ask for forgiveness. Reconciliation is in the air! And that's what good sermons are for: not pious words, but God-given messages which result in heartfelt action.

No one is pretending it's easy. I'll always remember a good friend of mine, who was director of a large mission compound with schools and a hospital and a church, saying to me: 'We've an American couple staying with us — delightful people. They're complete pagans, actually, but I can tell you that I'd rather be a castaway on a desert island with those two than with some of my missionary colleagues!' I can sympathise with him, but we are called to *love* our fellow-Christians, even if we don't like them; and God can give us the ability to do so.

There can only be true fellowship in a church if there is real reconciliation. The basic root of fellowship (*koinoia*) is 'sharing in', and so we are all sharing in the worship together, especially in the Communion service. But Paul would have us go further. He would say that we are all sharing in *Christ*. 'You are the body of Christ, and each one of you is a part of it.' (1 Corinthians 12:27.) Our fellowship means an interdependence in a truly spiritual sense, and by that very fact, we need to be 'at one' with one another. So our church life should have built-in opportunities for fellowship: weekly attendance at a church service is not enough, and a good church will make many and varied opportunities for extra fellowship meetings.

The author of the letter to the Hebrews puts it well: 'Let us consider how we may spur one another on towards love and good deeds. Let us not give up meeting together, as some are in the habit of doing, but let us encourage one another' (Hebrews 10:24-25.) Meeting together for mutual support and encouragement, and to 'spur one another towards love and good deeds', is a significant and important part of our worship. If there's no such meeting in your church or fellowship, then start one yourself. You've scriptural authority so to do – but don't forget to ask the minister first!

c) *Teaching*

Under the heading 'The Fellowship of Believers', the NIV New Testament paints this picture of the early church: 'They devoted themselves to the apostles' teaching and to the fellowship, to the breaking of bread and to prayer . . . praising God and enjoying the favour of all the people.' (see Acts 2:42-47.) The church 'enjoyed favour' and increased daily when it was a joyful gathering of Christians, before it became institutionalised. Would that it were thus today! We recognise the marks of this first-century church, for we should find them in our own prayers, breaking of bread, and fellowship.

But what about the apostles' teaching? My experience is that far too many Christians who fill the pews and seats of our churches week in and week out are ignorant of much basic Christian teaching. If asked to explain some of the great words of the New Testament: Grace, Justification, Sanctification, and Redemption, many would be floundering. Despite the fact that we in the West are richly endowed with translations of the Bible into contemporary English, to say nothing of modern worship songs and prayer books, there are many who are quite inarticulate about their faith. We expect school/Sunday School/Sabbath School to provide our children with a foundation in the great truths of our faith. But we need to build on the foundation we received.

The best way to do this, in my view, is by meeting together in a home and studying the New Testament ('the Apostles' Teaching') in fellowship. The small group Bible study is a sure, proven way of enabling believers 'to grow in the grace and knowledge of our Lord and Saviour Jesus Christ' (2 Peter 3:18). A dozen people (the optimum number), with a competent leader, all at different stages in their spiritual journey, sitting round studying the Scriptures together, with enough confidence in one another to admit, 'I don't understand this', or to ask 'What does that mean for me, today?' is a sure sign of a healthy church.

Some years ago as a lay pastor I was asked to develop the house groups in a large Anglican church. There were eight groups functioning, meeting weekly in various homes. By my visiting these groups, encouraging them, meeting with the leaders, providing them with study notes, and identifying potential new leaders, the numbers grew to twelve within a year – a 50% increase! As we encouraged church members to belong to a group, and to bring along their friends, so the groups grew and multiplied, about three or four being added each year, until after four or five years there were twenty-four groups functioning within the one parish. With between eight and twelve in each group, this meant there were 250 people who were 'growing in the grace and knowledge of their Lord and Saviour' – and the church was growing too. One lady, who'd become a Christian a few years earlier, told me: 'I don't mind missing church, but I hate to miss our home group meeting'! That's not quite what we intended, but it shows the great value of the home group as a place where people can feel secure among friends, and free to learn about and question their new-found faith. It shows, too, that the home group is a microcosm of the church itself.

For the home group is not just a meeting to study the Scriptures together. It is a fellowship gathering, so that when one member suffers, all suffer. It is a mutual support group, made up of people who pray for one another, who encourage one another, who help out other members. Sometimes a home group as an entity is asked to take on some task in the church: to lead evening worship, perhaps, or lead the prayers at the morning service, or to provide refreshments at a monthly meeting of all home group members. This knitting together of the body of Christ is a truly positive way of building up the church. And it certainly makes for more articulate Christians who know what they believe, and believe what they know.

A good test is to ask church members to state (or to write down) their answers to the question: 'What is the Gospel?' After all, we sing, 'We have a Gospel to proclaim, Good News for men o'er all the earth', and the world knows that the church's task is to 'preach the Gospel'. So every church member should be able to state clearly and confidently what the Gospel is. In my experience one gets many different answers, often poorly expressed. After some time in a home group, members should be clear in their minds as to what the Gospel is, and be able to express themselves with clarity and conviction.

The surest answer must be that found at the beginning of the 15th chapter of Paul's first letter to the Corinthians, and it is worth repeating in full.

'I want to remind you of the gospel I preached to you, which you received and on which you have taken your stand. By this gospel you are saved, if you hold firmly to the word I preached to you. Otherwise you have believed in vain.

'For what I received I passed on to you as of first importance: that Christ died for our sins according to the Scriptures, that he was buried, that he was raised on the third day according to the Scriptures, and that he appeared to Peter, and then to the Twelve. After that, he appeared to more than five hundred of the brothers at the same time, most of whom are still living, though some have fallen asleep. Then he appeared to James, then to all the apostles, and last of all he appeared to me also. . . . this is what we preach, and this is what you believed.' (1 Corinthians 15:1-8, 11.)

So the gospel is not only about the life of Jesus, not only about the teaching of Jesus, not only about the miracles of Jesus, not only about the healings of Jesus. What it is about mainly is the death and resurrection of Jesus, and it is 'according to the Scriptures'. The gospel focuses on the cross, and that deserves a section to itself.

2 The Cross

Few will deny that the cross is the central point of Christianity, not only its logo, but also its strength. Yet there are many who seek to avoid it, or at least evade it. Christianity is not about leading a clean and upright life while being kind, nice and tolerant to other people (a sort of humanism), though it should embrace this. It goes far deeper, and deals with the fundamental flaw at the heart of every human being: sin.

Sin is an unpleasant word, yet it is much misunderstood. Rugby football (and ice hockey) have a 'sin-bin' to which a player is sent for ten minutes if he has persistently committed a foul during the game — that is, if he has broken the rules of fair play. While it is true that sins are committed when we break God's commandments (see Exodus 20), sin (in the singular) is the basis of it all. For sin is living our lives without any reference to God; going our own way instead of trying to go his. Sin is acting as if God does not exist, ignoring him completely in our lives. From this basic sin come all the sins which, as the Bible says, 'so easily entangle us' (Hebrews 12.1).

The cross has the power to deal with this fundamental flaw in human nature. The writer to the Hebrews again: 'We have been made holy through the sacrifice of the body of Jesus Christ once for all.' (10:10.) The cross is the place where the 'sacrifice of the body of Jesus Christ' was made, which in God's eyes cancels out the sins of all those who come to the cross seeking forgiveness. It is not *automatically* for everybody, though it is for *all* people, everywhere. It is personal, and needs heartfelt repentance to become effective. So no one can ever say to another: 'Go to the cross', only 'come to the cross, for that's the place where I have found forgiveness, freedom from guilt, and new life!'

No wonder Paul – former Pharisee who persecuted Christians – could write: 'May I never boast except in the cross of our Lord Jesus Christ' (Galatians 6:14); and again, 'For the message of the cross is foolishness to those who are perishing, but to us who are being saved it is the power of God.' (1 Corinthians 1:18.) Christians should ever keep the cross central, not only to their faith but to their lives. For the power of the cross is that it can change our lives towards what God wants us to be.

The Archbishop of Paris was once preaching in Notre Dame Cathedral, and told this story: 'A good few years ago now, a couple of bored teenagers were fooling about in the square outside this cathedral. To have some fun, one of the lads suggested that they go to make a mock confession to the priest inside. So into the cathedral they went, and one of them knelt down by the confessional and reeled off a catalogue of misdeeds from the top of his head, while his friend stood back, laughing up his sleeve. But the wise old priest in the confessional realised that this was not a heartfelt repentance at all. So he came out from the box and said to the youth, "Before I can absolve you, there's just one thing you must do", and he marched him up to the altar. In the centre, surrounded by glittering candles and a gold reredos, was the figure of Christ on the cross. "Now," said the priest, "I want you to kneel down and look up at that figure on the cross, say to him what you've just confessed to me, and at the end say, 'but I don't care.'" The young man knelt down, and looked up at the figure of Christ crucified; he tried to speak, but no words came. Finally, he broke down in tears, and wept copiously. "That young man", concluded the Archbishop, "was me!"' Never underestimate the power of the cross to change lives.

Yet the cross is a source of power mainly, if not only, to those who trust in it and its efficacy; it is not a lucky charm to wear round someone's neck, presumably to ward off evil. Jesus once said, 'Just as Moses lifted up the snake in the desert, so the Son of Man must be lifted up, that everyone who believes in him may have eternal life.' (John 3:14-15.) What does this mean? 'The Son of Man' was Jesus' title for himself; so, when was Jesus lifted up? Surely, on the cross. But what does the reference to Moses have to do with it?

The story is found in the Book of Numbers. The Israelites were on their long journey to the promised land. They found a pleasant grassy plain after days in the desert wilderness, and eagerly pitched camp there. But the plain was alive with small poisonous snakes. Many folk were bitten, and some died. So the people came grumbling to Moses. 'We were better off as slaves in Egypt,' they said, 'rather than being bitten to death here.' Moses prayed to God for the people. God told him to make a bronze snake, and to put it up on a pole in the centre of the camp. Then anyone who was bitten could look up at that snake, be cured, and live. So Moses did just that, setting up this bronze snake on a stout pole in the middle of the encampment. He told the people that if they were bitten by a poisonous snake they only had to turn and look at the brass snake, and God promised that they would live (Numbers 21:4-9).

So let's imagine two men walking along a bush path near the camp. Suddenly they both get bitten by snakes. One says, 'Oh, quick, where's the bronze snake? I've only got to look at it and I'll be cured.' The other says, 'You don't believe that rubbish, do you? How can looking at a bronze snake cure you?' Two different reactions to the same problem. And what is the answer to the second man's question, anyway? Is it that a laser beam of anti-snake serum comes from the snake's eyes straight onto the bite that will cure it? Not at all. The reason for the cure is simple. The man who looks up at the snake is cured for one reason only: because God promised it, and he trusts God and his word. So to be healed of the snake's poisonous bite, you have to *turn* to the bronze snake, and *trust* in the God who said you'd be cured if you trusted.

Now in the Bible, from Genesis to Revelation, the snake is a symbol of sin. And the Bible teaches that we've all been bitten by the sin-snake. But Jesus promises that if we turn to him and trust in the cross, we will be healed; our sin will be forgiven, and we'll have the power of God to deal with it in our lives. We can of course ignore it, or rationalise that trusting in the cross (looking at the snake) cannot possibly help us. But we'll miss out on being reconciled to God, and knowing his inner peace in our lives. 'For God was pleased . . . through him [Christ] to reconcile to himself all things, whether things on earth or things in heaven, by making peace through his blood, shed on the cross.' (Colossians 1:19, 20.)

I was once at a gathering of Christian leaders where the speaker talked about the cross. He had a wooden cross on the table in front of him. We, his hearers, had come from far and wide, and so did not know one another. At the end of his talk the speaker invited us to write down our besetting sins, whether they be bad temper, lewd thoughts, resentment, bitterness – *whatever*. We then screwed up our piece of paper, went on our knees to the cross, and left the papers there. It was a most spiritually cleansing experience.

So what does the cross mean in your life? Is it a place you visit often? Have you taken on board completely the fact of Christ's forgiveness, so that there's 'no more guilt'? African Christians – who've had their share of suffering – used to say, 'No Cross – No Crown'. And Jesus himself said more than once, ' "If anyone would come after me, he must deny himself and take up his cross daily and follow me." ' (Luke 9:23; cf. Luke 14:27.) The fruitful and positive Christian disciple will be a cross-bearer, one who takes up his cross *daily*.

The cross, however, is only one side of the coin; the other is the resurrection. You can't have one without the other. With no resurrection, the cross is just the final end of a high-minded martyr; with no cross, the resurrection is like the reawakening of springtime, but without any spiritual renewal at all.

The glory of the cross is the fact that it's empty.

Many years ago I was doing some teaching practice in the east end of London. It was an RE lesson for pupils aged 11-12 or so, and we were looking at the different eye-witnesses' reactions to the cross of Christ. So I got the pupils to draw a full-length cross in their exercise books; then on the left-hand side we identified the different people present: the disciples, the Roman soldiers, the Scribes and Pharisees, the bystanders, etc. Opposite each group the pupils had to write down how they had reacted: for example, the disciples 'stood afar off'; the Roman soldiers gambled for his garments; and so on. One girl asked to draw a picture of Jesus on the cross, but I said, 'No'. She persisted, finally demanding, 'Why can't I draw a picture of Jesus on the cross?' I was anxious to continue with teaching, so I said I would tell her at the end of the lesson. As soon as the bell went, up she came demanding to know why I had not let her draw a picture of Jesus on the cross. 'Well, Maureen,' I replied, 'you see, the cross wasn't the end. Jesus rose from the dead, and is alive now. So we don't want to remember a dead Saviour, but a living Lord!' A huge glow spread over her face. 'Oh, I see,' she said thoughtfully. 'Yes, we don't want Jesus on the cross, 'cos he's alive!' It was a rare moment of delight, because I knew, that for one pupil at least, a great new truth had dawned.

The cross is central to the Christian faith, and our Lord and Master told his followers to take up their crosses daily. So ask yourself what it means to you that Jesus died on the cross *for you*. What does it mean to you that Jesus rose from the dead and is alive now, today, and forever? 'The message of the cross', wrote Paul, 'to us who are being saved, is the power of God.' Is it – for you – today?

chapter Seven

Living as the salt of the earth

For some years we have been leading pilgrimages to Israel/Palestine, 'the Land of the Holy One'. We always enjoy visiting Bethlehem, where we worship overlooking an area known as the Shepherds' Fields. In Manger Square there's an ancient church built over a cave, which tradition says is the birthplace of the infant Christ. It was built to focus on Jesus, and to venerate him. Yet in its way it has become a living parable.

For a start, you have to bend down to enter the church. The door is low and narrow, and it is necessary to stoop, and to enter one by one. Now *there's* a lesson, surely? It brings vividly to mind Jesus' words: 'I am the door; who-ever enters through me shall be saved.' (John 10:9, KJV.) And we can't enter and be saved just because our family, or our culture, is Christian; we have to enter on our own. And we can't enter boldly and proudly, but humbly, sub-missively, stooping into his presence.

But the door has not always been low and narrow. There's a much higher lintel, with the outline of two doors, now bricked in. When they were in use, the entrance to the church was abused. The larger doors were boarded up because men rode their horses inside, or camels drifted in, or even looters came with wagons to plunder the sacred place. Similarly, throughout history, the church has been abused by people who have wanted to use it for their own ends, and not as a place of worship.

Once we enter the cavernous building, the plinths of ancient pillars are shown, and a glass plate in the floor reveals mosaic tiling underneath. People are fascinated by the beauty of the past, but fail to focus on the Christ of the present. Moving further inside, one discovers three different altars, each belonging to a different denomination. I've been present when three different services were going on simultaneously, each apparently trying to outdo the others. Again, it's a lesson we need to heed: so many Christian Churches and organisations seem to be in competition with one another, rather than in co-operation. No one Christian group/church/fellowship has a monopoly on truth, or on the one and only way to worship or celebrate Communion. (Those with rigid views who doubt this should look carefully at Acts chapter ten, closely examining verses 1-4, 27-28, 34-35, 47-48.) If only we could swallow our pride, shed our inhibitions and prejudices, get back to the basics of the Gospel, and work alongside one another, maybe the world would sit up and take notice.

The Church of the Nativity in Bethlehem is a large building without pews, so the floor space is significant: it gives the impression of spreading out in all directions. There are ancient foundations, for the church has been destroyed and rebuilt. Here again is a parable: Christ's Church is spread out to the four corners of the globe. It is universal. It, too, has been persecuted almost into non-existence – almost, but not quite. The foundations are there, and will never be destroyed: 'the gates of hell shall not prevail against it'. Underneath the building which was created by human hands lies the crypt, a cave created by God's hand. This is the true foundation, the fundamental basis for all our faith, for all our worship: the place where Jesus, God's only Son, was born. It is when we deviate from the living Christ that difficulties arise; when we are distracted from the loving Lord that faith flounders.

The last time we visited the Church of the Nativity, my eye was caught by a man wandering around speaking animatedly into a mobile phone. Another facet of the parable: some people cannot put aside the gadgets of this world, even in a holy building, a sacred place. Of course, 'life must go on', but the whole point of stepping into a church (especially in Bethlehem) is to step aside from all worldly business and focus one's heart and mind on the things of God. Yet some seem unable to detach themselves from their own concerns to concentrate – even briefly – on God. So we positive people must never lose sight of our primary objective, our one true and only aim, which we should pursue with single-minded dedication – to worship Jesus, and him alone.

The most spiritual people I know are those who are focused on Jesus and who cultivate his presence daily in their lives. If Jesus really is God, and if the resurrection really is true (and Christianity affirms both), then we can and should know that the living Christ is with us day by day, as friend and guide, as strength and support, as we seek to live for him, and for him alone.

Now this is not to advocate a puritanical asceticism. Jesus affirmed that he came to offer us life, 'life in all its fullness'. This means we get involved in life, in society, seeking to meet the needs (as he did) of disadvantaged individuals, those handicapped physically, emotionally, materially, mentally. The Christian needs to be there among them, together with his Lord, acting in his name.

Equally, we should find life enjoyable. In *The Kingdom of*

God is a Party, Tony Campolo caricatures Christian groups who impose petty rules and restrictions on their adherents, all in the name of Christianity: no this, no that – despite the gospel records showing Jesus as a party man (John 2:1-10; Matthew 9:10, 14; *et al*).

But equally, we must never forget our first allegiance, our prime commitment. There are many self-centred Christians, with their own agenda instead of God's. Surely, the true meaning of 'the priesthood of all believers' is not that everyone is called to act as a priest, but that everyone is called to put God first, to obey his calling, to follow his will and purpose. Only thus can we become positive people; only thus can we become the 'salt of the earth'.

We need to remember at all times that we are citizens of the Kingdom of God; and this is a prior allegiance. Not many of us in the West have to face a conflict between allegiance to Christ and allegiance to the State. But many of our forebears did, and many of our fellow-Christians, living under totalitarian regimes, still do today. Yet in the West we see an increasingly secular society. As I write, this very morning's newspaper informs me that prayers are to be abolished at the Graduation ceremony of a major Scottish university, and also that a curriculum policy group has decreed that agnosticism and atheism should be taught in RE lessons. My paper comments that this is not just political correctness, but an attack on Christianity itself. The tentacles of secularism are squeezing out Christianity.

So, how do we keep faith with our citizenship in heaven? Surely by affirming and displaying Christian standards and Christian virtues, by seeking to live out the Christian life, and by supporting Christian institutions. I have a personal rule that of all the many requests for charitable giving that bombard me almost daily, I'll give only to Christian charities. I know that cancer research is eminently worth-while, that lifeboat men do a magnificent job, that foot and mouth painting artists need support. But they have the whole population to draw that support from. The Christian charities and Missions, by and large, have only the Christians to fund them – in Britain, about 10% of the population. So these are the ones that rely totally on the support of Christians, and these are the ones that have mine.

Again, we are amazed every year how many committed Christian friends use secular Christmas cards sold in chain stores to send their greetings. There are so many Christian charities which rely on Christians to help their income by purchasing their cards at Christmas. Non-Christians can, and do, buy the chain-store cards; I feel that Christians could and should buy Christian cards, preferably with a Christian picture, message, or text. Let's never forget that our citizenship is in heaven: let's exercise that privilege all we can.

As citizens of the Kingdom of God, then, we have obligations to perform and dues to pay. Our obligations are simply to offer ourselves to God, to ask him to use the gifts he's given us for his service. One person who did this was a serving girl, Gladys Aylward. At the time she was converted she was working as a maid for a well-known explorer. She knew in her heart that God was calling her to go to China as a missionary, but she hadn't the money, the training, or the resources. One evening in her attic bedroom she got down on her knees beside her bed, emptied onto the bed all the money she had in the world, together with her Bible, and prayed to God: 'Here's me, Lord. Here's my money; here's my Bible. Take us, Lord, take us and use us, O Lord.' Well, he did, and her achievements became famous. Books were written about her, she was entertained to tea by the Queen at Buckingham Palace, and her story was made into a Hollywood film. The actress portraying her (Ingrid Bergman) said that the hardest part to play was kneeling down and saying that prayer in the attic. Of course it was! You can't act that role; you can't pretend. It has to be for real, to give your life and all you have to God.

Yet it should be for real for every Christian. We offer God our time, our talents, and all we have. And then it's up to him how he uses them – and often it may surprise us. When I offered myself to God on a hillside near Keswick, I was amazed that he wanted me to become a missionary. In fact, I was somewhat disappointed: I didn't want to become a missionary at all. But the King had ordered it, and I'd committed myself (like any soldier) to obeying the King. So off I went, spent ten happy years in Africa, and formed some lifelong friendships. Thanks be to God!

If we are living in God's Kingdom, if we are living with the presence of Christ with us daily (whether we realise it or not), our lives should be characterised by joy. So positive Christians will see difficult times from God's perspective. They will count their blessings, not recount their grievances. The apostle Paul wrote a brief letter of just four chapters to the church at Philippi in which the notion of joy or rejoicing is reiterated no fewer than sixteen times. Yet when he wrote it Paul was actually imprisoned. His dire circumstances meant nothing; his living Lord meant everything. Someone has analysed the four chapters of Philippians as Joy in suffering (chapter 1), Joy in serving (2), Joy in believing (3), and Joy in giving (4); these are not the usual things we rejoice over, but the captive Paul did!

Living as the salt of the earth is a lifelong commitment,

and a daily commitment as well. These aren't my words; they are the words of Jesus to those who would follow him, to every disciple: 'He [Jesus] said to them *all*, "If anyone would come after me, he must deny himself and take up his cross *daily* and follow me." ' (Luke 9:23, *my italics*.) It's a tough assignment, and we all fall short; yet it's what we are called to, and as we are called, so we are equipped. It's bound to lead to change: changes in our lifestyle, our habits, our priorities. In fact, we should be concerned if following Christ does *not* lead to our changing our ways.

Some of the most powerful Christians who live out their faith daily are those who have been changed dramatically. I've met a former prostitute who's now a Christian minister; we've talked to a violent prisoner who's now a persuasive preacher. But most of us are ordinary people living decent lives. What can God do with us (not 'for us'; the creature cannot dictate to the Creator)? That great Christian apologist C. S. Lewis put it this way:

'The more we get what we now call "ourselves" out of the way and let him take us over, the more truly ourselves we become. . . . it's no good trying to "be myself" without him. The more I resist him and try to live on my own, the more I become dominated by my own heredity and upbringing and surroundings and natural desires.' (*Mere Christianity*, pages 185-6.)

And this, of course, expands the words of Jesus which follow on from those quoted above: ' "Whoever wants to save his life will lose it, but whoever loses his life for me will save it. What good is it for a man to gain the whole world, and yet lose or forfeit his very self?" ' (Luke 9:24.) Sometimes this is encapsulated in the epigram: 'Let go and let God', which sounds easy (and rather smug), but is still pretty difficult. Yet it affirms a great truth.

It is we ourselves whom God wants. He wants you and me, with all our quirky ways and quaint habits. Christianity is not a matter of God calling us to do good deeds in his name, but of God calling ordinary (and bad) people to live for him. But he wants all of me, all of you, with all our gifts and goodness, and all our faults and failings. And he accepts us as we are, 'warts and all'. To quote C. S. Lewis again, because he puts it so much better than I can:

'Christ says, "Give me all. I don't want so much of your time and so much of your money and so much of your work; I want you. I have not come to torment your natural self, but to kill it. No half-measures are any good. I don't want to cut off a branch here and a branch there. I want to have the whole tree down. I don't want to drill the tooth, or crown it, or stop it, but to have it out. Hand over the whole natural self, all the desires which you think innocent as well as the ones you think wicked – the whole outfit. I will give you a new self instead. In fact, I will give you Myself; my own will shall become yours."' (*Mere Christianity*, page 162.)

That's how we can become positive people. That's how we can live as 'salt of the earth'.

chapter

Praying positively

No book on discipleship, on learning to 'grow in the grace and knowledge of our Lord Jesus Christ', can ignore the vital topic of prayer. Yet many avowed Christians have a weak prayer life, and are content to paddle in the shallows rather than launch out into the deep.

We all need to grow in our prayer life. Even the twelve apostles, when they saw Jesus praying, said, 'Lord, teach us to pray', and his answer was to teach them the prayer best known throughout Christendom, called the Lord's Prayer. (More accurately, it should be called 'the Disciples' Prayer' for it is the prayer he taught his *followers* to pray; the true Lord's Prayer — the heartfelt prayer of Jesus to his Father — can be found in John's gospel, chapter 17.) Countless people pray the Lord's Prayer every day world-wide. I wonder how many people notice the number of times it contains the words 'I' or 'me'. Not once! This prayer is God-focused, not about self. 'Thy (or 'your') will be done'; 'Thy Kingdom come.' 'Thine is the glory.' There is a sandwich in-between, when we ask for *our* daily needs (not wants): 'Give *us* this day *our* daily bread' and to be kept strong in the faith: 'Lead us not into temptation, but deliver *us* from evil.' Whereas our prayers are so often self-centred, this prayer is wholly God-focused. (See Matthew 6:9-13.)

So how do we grow in our prayer life? When do we start making prayer an important part of our lives, not just something tacked on when we have time? I chuckled, almost scoffed, when my wife prayed at the cot of our firstborn, just a few days old. 'What are you doing?' said I, ever the pragmatic male. 'He doesn't understand at all.'

'Well,' she replied, 'when *do* you start praying for him? When he's two, three, five years old?'

I was justly rebuked. Again, married Christian couples should always make time to pray aloud *together* each morning or bedtime. Thus their joint commitment to God and to his service will cement their commitment to each other. For the follower of Jesus, prayer should be as much a part of the daily routine as having a meal. Prayer is a great privilege, and a deeper understanding of prayer will help us to develop the quality of our prayer life, to pray positively.

The privilege of prayer

Just as the body needs air to breathe and food to eat in order to sustain its physical life, so the soul needs prayer ('pray without ceasing') as its air, and Bible reading ('desire the sincere milk of the word') as its food, to sustain the spiritual life. The hymn-writer James Montgomery wrote, 'Prayer is the soul's sincere desire, uttered or unexpressed. . . . Prayer is the Christian's vital breath, the Christian's native air', and thus it is. Not a chore, but a joy; not a duty, but a privilege.

We pray because Jesus told us to, and Jesus taught us to. In his famous Sermon on the Mount, Jesus told us: 'When you pray, go into your room, close the door and pray to your Father.' (Matthew 6:6.) Get in touch with God, and he'll be in touch with you. Open yourself to him, for it's just between you and him. And he wants the real 'you', without pretence or any mask. But Jesus didn't just tell us to pray; he taught us by example, by exemplifying the life of prayer: 'Very early in the morning, while it was still dark, Jesus got up, left the house and went off to a solitary place where he prayed.' (Mark 1:35.) The whole Bible, especially the New Testament, sees prayer as essential to any spiritual life, and a vital part of our growth as Christians. To be in direct communication with our heavenly Father is a privilege which we should be constantly using. But perhaps first we should try to understand what prayer is all about.

The purpose of prayer

If we believe that God is in control of the universe, and if we have handed over our lives to him so that he is in the driving seat, then prayer naturally follows, as we seek his guidance and direction for our lives, and show our dependence on him. So prayer is not making a bargain with God ('If you do this for me, God, then I'll go to church for the next month'!), nor is it trying to twist God's arm to do something he seems reluctant to do. It's not seeking to recruit or persuade him to act on our behalf, though many people's personal prayers would suggest that it is. Prayer is simply seeking to align oneself with God's will: not what I want, but what he wants.

There are some remarkable verses about prayer tucked away in John's gospel, where Jesus initially asks for himself, then rejects his own prayer. ' "Now is my heart troubled, and what shall I say? 'Father, save me from this hour?' No, it was for this very reason I came to this hour. Father, glorify your name." ' (John 12:27, 28.)

I believe these two verses show us the core of prayer: not to ask for self, but to ask that God's name is glorified, whatever that means, whatever that costs. So often our prayers are, 'Father, help me out of this trouble; Father, save me from this situation; Father, get me out of this mess.'

Recently, our son was badly injured in a road accident. We prayed earnestly for his healing, both physically and emotionally. The prayer certainly accelerated the healing, for which we give glory to God.

A few years ago we were buying a new house that was being built. We put down a token reserve payment, but the day came when we had to put down a 10% deposit – a considerable sum to us – by the deadline date. Our solicitor rightly told us very emphatically not to pay the deposit until our own house had been contractually sold. We had no buyer by the deadline date, and asked for an extension. We were given ten days. We had prayed about the buying of the new house, and God had shown us (by two signs) that it was right. So we redoubled our prayers about the selling of the old house, and we had a definite buyer the day before the deadline date. We phoned the estate agent to tell him a cheque was in the post. He was amazed: 'How did you manage that?' he asked. 'We prayed about it,' we responded – a response he was surprised to hear – *but God was honoured!*

There's a possible objection here that some may make, which would go something like this. 'Well, if God really loves me and really wants the best for me, why did he allow me to lose my job/suffer this illness/get into such a bad situation?' The short answer is that trusting God is not an insurance policy; not a shield against the 'slings and arrows of outrageous fortune'. Being a Christian does not mean we automatically become immune to tragedy and disaster, to illness and disease. If it did, imagine the vast numbers who would jump on the Christian bandwagon just to immunise themselves from hardship and suffering!

Consider this: a tower block has a raging fire on the twenty-first floor, and thirty-seven people are trapped there, seven of whom are Christians. Is God going to pluck those seven to safety, and let the other thirty be burnt to death just because they don't believe in him? I don't think I could worship that sort of God.

Anyway, how do you define 'Christian'? We are all, each one of us, at different stages on our journey in the Christian faith. We all live in the world, and we are all subject to the trials and hardships and tough times that living in the world involves. A faith in God, however strong, does not immunise us from the traumas and accidents of life. Our family suffered four hammer-blows of life in a decade, including the death of our son (a Christian) at the age of 27. Yet we did not once feel like blaming God; indeed, God drew very close to us, and we were borne up on the prayers of his people.

When we pray, we come to a God who wants to bless us, who wants the best for us, just as a proud father wants the best for his children. He longs for us – with all our complex characteristics, all our hang-ups and inhibitions, with all our baggage of culture and nurture – to be 'conformed to the image of his Son'. We come to a God who wants us to show our dependence upon him, so that he can work out his purposes in us and through us. So an essential element of prayer is being open to God, allowing him to 'work in us what is pleasing to him' (Hebrews 13:21). Prayer is not coming to God with a shopping list of our requests; rather, it is beseeching God to put the brilliant searchlight of his blessing upon a situation, an individual, a group, an undertaking – and all to *his* glory.

Although we pray 'Almighty God', I believe that God limited this 'almighty' power according to the prayers of his people. 'You do not have, because you do not ask God.' (James 4:2.) He has given everyone free will, and he respects that and won't override it or veto it. Because he has given us free will, he has thereby curtailed his own freedom to act. But our prayers will release his power, and bring it to bear on the object of our prayers. This is a very sobering thought, and is why prayer is so vital. If we withhold our prayers, we are withholding God's power in the world; we are blocking his blessing. Then licentiousness is given free play, and thus the freedom to sin, to do evil, to commit gross wrong.

Prayer is such a vital force for good that we must use it positively as much as we can. No wonder Paul says 'Pray without ceasing' and 'Pray at all times'!

The power of prayer

'The prayer of a righteous man [person] is powerful and effective,' wrote James in his letter (5:16), and it's the adjectives that are important. We are 'righteous' not because of our good deeds but because we are born again into Christ, and thus are clothed with *his* righteousness. But how can our prayer become 'powerful and effective'? It's all too easy to slip into a repetitive routine, which can become a rut. And we can only pray truly when we have a living, loving relationship with our Father-God. Even just calling God 'our Father' indicates a relationship, and implies that we are his dependent children. So let us come to him in expectancy, as children, wanting to tell 'Daddy' all about our joys and sorrows, our hopes and fears, our worries and concerns; just wanting to share them with him. Prayer then will be from our hearts, not from our lips alone (see

Isaiah 29:13). So to make our prayers more potent, may I suggest some guidelines, a six-point programme in the school of prayer.

1) *Be persistent*

Immediately after the disciples had asked Jesus to teach them to pray, and he'd responded with the 'Lord's Prayer', he told them a tale: 'If any of you has a friend, and you go to him in the middle of the night and say, "Lend me three loaves, my dear fellow, for a friend of mine has just arrived after a journey and I've no food to put in front of him"; and then he answers from inside the house, "Don't bother me with your troubles. The front door is locked, and my children and I have gone to bed. I simply cannot get up now and give you anything!" Yet, I tell you, that even if he won't get up and give him what he wants simply because he is his friend, yet if he persists, he will rouse himself and give him everything he needs. And so, I tell you, ask and it will be given you.' (Luke 11:5-10, Phillips.)

It is Jesus who tells us to be persistent in prayer, to go on asking. A commentator on Luke's gospel makes this point: 'Persistence (or boldness) in prayer overcomes our insensitivity, not God's. To practise persistence does more to change our hearts and minds than his, and it helps us to understand and express the intensity of our need. Persistence in prayer helps us to recognise God's work.' (*Life Application Bible*.)

There's a lovely story in the Old Testament which perfect-ly illustrates this, and also reinforces our belief that prayer releases God's power in a situation. It's worth quoting in full.

'The Amalekites came and attacked the Israelites at Rephidim. Moses said to Joshua, "Choose some of our men and go out to fight the Amalekites. Tomorrow I will stand on top of the hill with the staff of God in my hands." So Joshua fought the Amalekites as Moses had ordered, and Moses, Aaron and Hur went to the top of the hill. As long as Moses held up his hands, the Israelites were winning, but whenever he lowered his hands, the Amalekites were winning. When Moses' hands grew tired, they took a stone and put it under him and he sat on it. Aaron and Hur held his hands up − one on one side, one on the other − so that his hands remained steady till sunset. So Joshua overcame the Amalekite army with the sword. . . . Moses built an altar and called it The Lord is my Banner. He said, "For hands were lifted up to the throne of the Lord"' (Exodus 17:8-13, 15-16a).

Let us be equally persistent in lifting up our hands in prayer to the throne of the Lord. Persistence pays!

2) *Be pointed*

It's fairly easy to pray 'blanket' prayers: 'O Lord, feed the starving in Africa' or 'O God, make wars to cease in all the world.' But it's far better to pray targeted prayers: 'O Lord, assist the aid workers seeking to feed those starving in the Sudan.' So be specific in your praying, rather than general.

Joshua had to learn this lesson. After capturing Jericho in dramatic fashion − by marching around the walls for seven days, as God had ordered, until the walls caved in − he sent a part of his army (just 2,500 men) to capture Ai, a small hilltop town. But they were defeated. Joshua repented and 'fell face down before the Lord, remaining until evening' (persistence!). But God told him to stand up, and said that there was 'sin in the camp'. Joshua rooted out the sin, and then the Lord instructed him to capture Ai by laying an ambush, using his whole army of 30,000 men.

However, the Lord told Joshua that he was not to lead the army himself, but ' "Hold out towards Ai the javelin that is in your hand, for into your hand I will deliver the city." So Joshua held out his javelin towards Ai. . . . Joshua did not draw back the hand that held out his javelin until he had destroyed . . . Ai.' (Joshua 8:18, 26.)

Is not this a lesson in targeting our prayers? Joshua's javelin had no military significance at all; in the battle, it was useless. But it was pointed constantly at the enemy stronghold, directing God's power on that target. And so he was victorious. A valuable lesson in directly pointing our prayers onto a situation, a person, a condition, or indeed an enemy stronghold.

3) *Be patient*

Anyone who has progressed just a little way in the school of prayer knows that sometimes the answer seems a long time coming; and sometimes our prayers are not answered at all. When Terry Waite, the Archbishop of Canterbury's envoy, was kidnapped and imprisoned in Beirut in the 80s, prayers were made daily for him by many people around the world; yet it was five years before he was released. And if a prayer is not granted, it may well be that the answer is 'No'. Paul said, 'Three times I pleaded with the Lord to take it [a thorn in the flesh] away from me. But he said to me, "My grace is sufficient for you, for my power is made perfect in weakness." ' (2 Corinthians 12:8-9.)

Quite often we have found that people who come to a living faith in Jesus Christ have had someone praying for them over a period of time — sometimes for years. We were friendly with a girl who'd become a Christian, whose husband was really a ne'er-do-well. He gambled and drank away any money he'd earned, but he was touched by his wife's conversion. I befriended him, and we spent time together on a number of occasions. Suddenly and dramatically he became a Christian, phoning me at 6am one day to say so. When we met, he said, 'It's like life has suddenly changed from being in black and white to being in colour.' He instantly gave up gambling and drinking, started to repay his debts, and to look after his family. I asked him, 'Billy, have you ever had any Christian input at all?' He replied, 'As a boy, I used to visit my grandmother. She'd read me a Bible story, and pray for me. She once told me that she'd pray for me every day.' So her prayers were answered – eventually! Remember Tennyson's words: 'More things are wrought by prayer than this world dreams of.'

4) *Be practical*

When I was a student I was suddenly and surprisingly made Missionary Secretary of the Christian Union. As such, I was praying for men and women to serve God in the hospitals and schools of Africa, and encouraging my fellow students to apply for such posts. One day God showed me, to my great surprise, that he wanted me to go and teach in Northern Nigeria. In other words, I was to be an answer to my own prayers!

We can't expect God to do it all while we sit back and do nothing. It's little use praying for the starving in the Sudan unless we are prepared to give a decent donation to those organisations – Tear Fund, ADRA, Cafod, Christian Aid – seeking to relieve those who are suffering.

When Jesus put some mud on the eyes of the man born blind, he told him, 'Go and wash in the pool of Siloam.' Now the man may have thought, 'What good will that do? I've been blind all my life, and I'll stay blind; washing in the pool of Siloam won't help me to see.' Fortunately, he did go and wash, and his sight was restored. Then he had a real story to tell: 'One thing I know: before, I was blind, now I can see.' (John 9:1-25.)

5) *Be perceptive*

In Shakespeare's play, *Hamlet, Prince of Denmark,* the young prince prepares to kill his uncle Claudius whom he strongly suspects of murdering his father in order to marry Hamlet's mother. He goes to Claudius's bedroom with a dagger, but Claudius is kneeling down, praying. Hamlet decides he cannot kill a man at his prayers. So he leaves. Claudius rises from his knees and says: 'My words fly up, my thoughts remain below; Words without thoughts never to Heaven go.'

I would suggest that we've all been there: our lofty words are divorced from our earthbound thoughts, and concentration goes out of the window. So we need to think ourselves into our prayers, to use our minds as much as our lips, to make sure our words are accompanied by our thoughts.

It's not much good praying if you don't believe that God will hear your prayer. It's not much better if you don't believe that God will answer your prayer. You must be convinced that God will answer your prayer in his own way and at his own time.

So prayer must be sincere and genuine, heartfelt and unselfish. If prayer is aligning ourselves with God's will in order to do what he wants, instead of trying to get him to do what we want, then our petitions will be unselfish. And the best way to concentrate the mind is to use Scripture. Read a passage of Scripture — a parable, or an incident from the gospels, a section from an epistle, or some verses from the Psalms – and turn what you read into prayer. Is there a message for me in this Scripture passage – someone I need to forgive, something I have to act upon, someone I need to pray for? Using the Scriptures in our prayer time can aid the concentration wonderfully.

6) *Be praising*

The Christian is called to 'live to the *praise* of God's glory', and that should be the aim of all our praying, the motivating theme of our prayer life. As evidence I simply ask, 'How does the Lord's Prayer end?' 'Thine be the glory'! That alone should teach us to praise God for his glory.

We need to learn to praise God whatever the circum-stances. The Romanian pastor Richard Wurmbrand tells how he was so overcome by the presence of God in his prison cell – where he'd been put solely because he was a Christian minister – that he sang and danced so much that the guards told him to keep quiet! It is a great gift to sing God's praise at all times and in all situations, and we'll grow nearer to God when we learn to do so. Surely the hymn-writer got it right:

'Fill thou my life, O Lord my God, in every part with praise,
That my whole being may proclaim thy being and thy ways.

'Praise in the common things of life, its goings out and in;
Praise in each duty and each deed, however small and mean.

'Fill every part of me with praise: Let all my being speak
Of thee and of thy love, O Lord, poor though I be, and weak.

'So shalt thou, Lord, receive from me the praise and glory due;
And so shall I begin on earth the song forever new.'

Horatius Bonar (1808-1889).

A song of praise can transform the dullest life!

Praising God is one way in which we 'glorify his name', acknowledging that he is the source of our joy. Once Jesus sent out 72 of his disciples on a mission (Luke 10:1ff). When they returned with joy at the power of God, we read that 'Jesus, full of joy through the Holy Spirit, said, "I praise you, Father, Lord of heaven and earth, because you have hidden these things from the wise and learned, and revealed them to little children. Yes, Father, this was your good pleasure." ' (v. 21.)

Jesus is praising God – and so should we! The writer of that old and lovely hymn knew what he was singing about:

> 'Praise, my soul, the King of heaven!
> To his feet thy tribute bring;
> ransomed, healed, restored, forgiven,
> who like me his praise should sing?'
>
> *H. F. Lyte (1793-1847).*

We should thank God daily for the cross, praise him daily for Jesus, for have we not been 'ransomed, healed, restored, forgiven'? Keep a spirit of praise in your heart, and remember to thank him for answers to prayer. A praising person is always positive: a positive person is always praising.

One more thing: don't forget to thank God for the answers when they come. If you pray for your worship service (as you ought), remember to thank God for all you've received from it, be it the worship, the message, or the fellowship. Thankfulness in prayer helps us to grow in our prayer life. Remember the ten leprosy sufferers. Only one returned to give thanks, and Luke adds pointedly, '*he was a Samaritan*' (Luke 17:16, our emphasis). Thankfulness is only courtesy, and it acknowledges God's part in our prayer life. Paul puts it strongly: 'Give thanks in all circumstances, for this is God's will for you in Christ Jesus.' (1 Thessalonians 5:18.) It's a wonderful lesson to learn.

The promise

Is prayer a last resort, or a first priority? It's more likely to become the latter if you feel it's worthwhile, if you feel your prayers are answered. I like the story of the hardened journalist who once asked Archbishop William Temple if it really made any difference if he prayed. 'Well,' replied the Archbishop with a twinkle in his eye, 'I find that when I pray, coincidences happen!'

We need to hold on to those great promises that God has given us in Scripture, and even claim them for ourselves. 'Ask and it will be given to you; seek, and you will find; knock and the door will be opened to you.' (Luke 11:9.) Our loving Father wants the best for his children, as any good father would. And Jesus told us to *ask* for the best. If we are going to grow in our Christian lives, then we need the Holy Spirit, and the gifts that the Holy Spirit brings. So Jesus says to his followers: 'If you then, though you are evil, know how to give good gifts to your children, how much more will your Father in heaven give the Holy Spirit to those who ask him!' (Luke 11:13.) Have *you* asked him yet for this truly great gift? Let's make sure that we claim the promise that Jesus gave us, by asking to be filled with his Holy Spirit.

The whole message of this chapter can be summed up in two verses from the pen of Paul: 'We constantly pray for you, that our God may count you worthy of his calling, and that by his power he may fulfil every good purpose of yours and every act prompted by your faith. We pray this so that the name of our Lord Jesus may be glorified in you, and you in him, according to the grace of our God and the Lord Jesus Christ.' (2 Thessalonians 1:11, 12.)

chapter

Salt
in old age

We often hear, quite rightly, about the importance of a *lively* youth programme in our churches. Presenting the Gospel and winning young people for Christ is one of the most rewarding, and justly high-profile ministries that we undertake. But let's not ignore the other end of the spectrum, the elderly, for they too are the salt of the earth.

Quite often, some of the most active people in the church are the elderly. Perhaps because they have more time and less pressure; maybe because they are recently retired or widowed, they throw themselves wholeheartedly into church life – and how valuable they are!

But there can be sticking points. It is often thought that it is the elderly who object to change; that they are content with things as they are, so that any change will be seen as a threat to their security, to the ordered, familiar way of doing things. Yet this is not invariably the case. In my own church the average age is nearer 70 than 50, and a number are saying, 'We can't go on as we are; we must change our style of worship so that it is more appealing to a greater number.'

Older people and change

Older people often see the need for change, and are prepared to adapt to it, provided it is handled with sensitivity and consideration, and not thrust upon them without warning. As a Reader, I was once told by my Anglican minister, 'It's no good trying to do anything new or to change things; these people are completely passive, and just want to have things as they have always had them.' This seemed to me to be false theology – God is ever our contemporary – and what needed changing was that vicar's negative mindset. So I took his comment not as an instruction but as a challenge, and set out to prove him wrong.

The plain fact is that as people grow older, as friends, relatives and contemporaries begin to die, matters of life and death become more pressing. Their thoughts, rarely expressed, turn towards God, to the questions of life and death, to heaven and eternity. Thus the elderly are more open than ever to a clear presentation of the Gospel, which focuses on and addresses these issues.

It has been my privilege (in my old age) to be called to this ministry to the elderly, an experience I have found very rewarding. Many older people are open to new ideas, even to change in familiar worship patterns. And this is true of non-churchgoers, too; they are open to the Gospel, and helping them to a living faith in Christ is a great joy. Here are three stories, and each one has a lesson to teach us.

'Kay' was in her 80s and living alone. She had not been to church for forty years, but felt an urge to seek God. She wrote to five churches in the area (a determined woman!) asking for information about their worship and activities in her search for God. Two did not reply (can you believe it?), two sent her the times of their services, and one sent round the curate. He chatted and arranged to take her to the following Sunday's service, one for the whole family.

But that proved to be too much of a culture shock after forty years' absence. People were milling about, laughing and chatting, when she expected an atmosphere of reverence and quiet awe. Then the music started, not the stately organ, but guitars and drums. There was no robed choir, no robed minister, but a 'worship leader'. This can't be 'church', she thought. She couldn't make head or tail of the service. As she went out, a lady worshipper noticed she was new. 'We hope you'll come again,' she said brightly. 'You'll never see me here again,' Kay tartly retorted.

But perseverance paid off. She was visited again, and taken to the church's weekly luncheon club, which she much appreciated. Then she was taken to the traditional service ('that's better!'), and finally was brought to an Alpha course, which I happened to be running. In the small group discussion she felt cut off, isolated, but felt able to express it. 'I'm not one of you,' she said. 'I don't belong, do I?' She left, vowing never to come again. The next day the Lord prompted me to visit her. She was a little flustered when I arrived unexpectedly on the doorstep, but received me warmly, if somewhat apprehensively. We chatted together, and she unburdened herself, telling me that she wanted seriously to find God again.

'You said yesterday,' I ventured, 'that you felt you didn't belong. Do you *want* to belong?'

'Yes, I do,' she replied earnestly. A brief explanation of the way of salvation was followed by a prayer of commitment together. It was very real and genuine.

'Now you belong,' I said with a smile.

'Yes,' she responded, 'I really belong!'

Church worship (in the traditional style) is now real and meaningful to Kay, and she soon became a member of a home group. At the Alpha supper at the end of the course she brought five of her friends. When I visit her at home she tells me that she may be alone, but she's not lonely, because Jesus is with her, and she talks with him. At her request we were able to buy her a Bible, light and flexible enough for her arthritic hands, which she treasures.

The Lord had stirred in her heart a real desire to seek him. Despite a few awkward moments on the way, when she found him she fully embraced him, and he has meant everything to her in the twilight of her life.

Elderly encounter Jesus

'Bill' was one of those people who sit passively in the pews fairly regularly, yet never do much else in church life, and certainly never expresses their feelings or their faith. Bill was getting on in years, and church attendance became less regular. His wife came whenever she could, and he sometimes accompanied her. When an Alpha course was announced, it rang a bell with him; his daughter had been urging him to join such a course, and so he came somewhat reluctantly. About halfway through the course the scales fell from his eyes; he saw Jesus clearly, and took him into his life.

It made all the difference. Suddenly, Bill loved to read his Bible ('It's really come alive, Douglas!') and attend prayer meetings; truly disappointed if his ill-health meant he had to miss church. All this amounted to a change of lifestyle to which he had easily adjusted at the age of 76. At an area Alpha meeting he gave his testimony, 'I've sat in church services most of my life, and only now has it become real. I'm just beginning to learn what it is all about. For most of my life, the door to Christianity was open this much' (hands held chest high about three inches apart) (now it's *this* much!' (arms wide open). When Bill died in hospital a few years later, I was present, with his wife and daughter. I prayed with them just before he died, which he did with a serene smile on his face.

Baptism in old age

'Doris' was brought up as a believer and a church attender, but after marriage found the distraction of family life and running a home all-consuming, with no time for church. Her husband was a baptised church member and went to church on an irregular basis. She was 77 when he died suddenly and she was quite bereft. Loneliness set in, and she thought that, as a baptised believer, he'd be saved, whereas she wouldn't. She couldn't bear the thought of being separated from him, and felt that she had to be baptised too, if only in order to be with him in heaven.

It took her a week to summon up the courage to ring the church office and ask for baptism. She was advised to come to divine service and see the minister. Nervous and apprehensive, she slipped into the back row. Afterwards she spoke to my wife, but was so overcome with emotion that she broke down in tears.

It was arranged that we would both go and visit her in her home during the week. When we went and enquired why she wanted baptism, the reply was clear: 'It's my passport to heaven, isn't it? If I'm baptised, I'll go to heaven and be with my beloved husband.' We had to explain that there was more to it than that, that baptism signified an acceptance of Christian faith and belief.

'Well,' she retorted, 'if I go across to France, I just show my passport and they let me in.'

'Yes,' I replied, and with an inspired thought added, 'but you've got to be a citizen of your own country first to be eligible for your passport.'

She thought for a moment: 'Yes, I agree with that.'

'Well, you have to be a committed member of your church before you're baptised.'

'I see; what does that mean?'

'It means a brief period of instruction; it can be here, in your own home, just one to one.'

She melted, agreed, and we arranged another meeting to discuss basic Christian teaching. At the door she called out, 'Don't think you're going to change my lifestyle in any way – like coming to church every week – that's not for me.' The Lord sealed our lips; *we* were not going to change her lifestyle, but the Lord might.

The next time I went alone, and explained basic Christian teaching which she readily received and accepted. On leaving, I left her *Journey into Life*, saying that this would put clearly what I had been saying, and arranged to come again. The following week both my wife and I went, and on our arrival she flung open the door, and with a beaming face declared, 'I've prayed the prayer. I found my faith'!

As we talked, there was no doubt that she had come to a real and deep experience of the Lord. Soon she was baptised, and became an active church worker, despite her age. She helped with Alpha suppers, with the weekly church lunches (for the elderly), with church cleaning, and attended both weekend and mid-week services, as well as Ladies' meetings. When she had flu her daughter phoned me to ask me to convince her mother that she was *not* indispensable to the running of church activities! Then she joined our Pilgrimage to Israel, which was a real high spot for her. She planned to come again, but sadly died before it took place. We didn't try to change her lifestyle, but the Lord in his graciousness did, and she truly became the 'salt of the earth'.

The Lord loves the elderly. It was the dying Simeon and 84-year-old Anna who first recognised the baby Jesus as their Saviour when he was brought for naming at eight days of age (Luke 2:2-38). Given that elderly people are a significant proportion of society today, as well as a large majority in most of our churches, we should ensure that they are not neglected or taken for granted in our ministry. Pastoral care and 'being bothered with' are keys to opening up elderly people to the Gospel, as well as giving them a feeling that they belong and have a useful service to contribute to church life. We neglect the ministry to the elderly at our peril – and theirs; they, too, are the salt of the earth.

chapter Ten

Staying positive when life is negative

Rudyard Kipling began his famous poem 'IF' with these lines,

'If you can keep your head when all about you
Are losing theirs and blaming it on you . . .'

And it applies to the Christian, too. Can we hold fast to faith when our lives are crumbling all around us? Can we remain positive when everything is negative? Can we cope with difficulties, disease, and disasters occurring in our lives? As the old hymn put it: 'Will your anchor hold in the storms of life?' I have to say that our faith/anchor is not worth much unless it does. It must be pretty puny and feeble if it cannot cope with the trials and tribulations of 'outrageous fortune'. Handing over our lives to Jesus is no guarantee that we shall sail serenely through this earthly existence. We may have one foot in heaven, but we also have one foot on earth, and so we are subject, like everyone else, to the dangers and difficulties of daily living.

Good God. Bad World. Why?

Yet this poses a question which many find hard to face, let alone answer. Put in its simplest terms it is this: 'Why do bad things happen to good people?' But this is nothing new. One thousand years before Christ, the Psalmist was complaining, 'Why do the wicked flourish?' (Psalm 94:3;

37:35; see also Jeremiah 12:1.) Basically, the problem is this: if we have handed our lives over to God, and he is all-loving and all-powerful, why doesn't he look after his own? Why does he allow his people to suffer so much? It's worth exploring an answer.

First, we have to repeat: we must remember our dual citizenship all the time. As well as being citizens of God's Kingdom, we are citizens of this world. And in this world life is grossly unfair. The wicked often flourish; the righteous frequently lose out. And all of us are subject to the changes and chances of this life. We are a part of mankind, and subject to all the illnesses, diseases, accidents, wars, storms – everything that afflicts mankind.

Our faith in God, our being born into God's new family, is not an insurance policy which protects us from any of those things which afflict and affect the whole of mankind. Yet we sometimes think it should! 'Why should this happen to me?' people sometimes moan. Well, why shouldn't it? 'What have I done to deserve this?' is another cry. But bad things happen to most people, and our Christian faith doesn't guarantee immunity from their happening to us. If it did, of course, thousands upon thousands of people would jump on the Christian bandwagon for totally selfish reasons; self-protection from life's problems, immunity from life's hard knocks.

So we need to distinguish between God (who is absolute love, who is justice, mercy and compassion) and life (which is unfair, unjust, often callous and 'nasty, brutish, and short' as the philosopher Thomas Hobbes put it). But this is *not* to say that God is not a part of life, or is aloof and indifferent to us. The Christian faith affirms most strongly that God not only loves us, is most interested in us, and cares about us, but that he even came down to earth to share human existence with us.

Jesus himself was not immune from the harsh climate of the human condition. Consider what he endured: he was a refugee, homeless, misunderstood by parents and family, solitary, accused of being a liar and in league with the devil, hungry, beaten up, unjustly accused, unfairly treated and punished, rejected, mocked and jeered at, forsaken by all his closest friends, betrayed by a colleague, and crucified.

If you feel life's treated you unfairly, if you feel bitter and resentful about your hurts and unjust treatment, consider Jesus! Even before the terrible degradation and awful agony of the cross, Jesus had experienced most of the deprivations of life. Bad things certainly happened to this most righteous of all people. William Temple wrote, 'Men say, "If God really loved this world, he'd do something about it." The Christian points to Jesus, and says, "He did; He did." Then men say, "If God looked down on this world, with all its pain and suffering, its sin and sordidness, its agony and anguish, its lust and greed, its wickedness and evil, its terrible injustices, he'd do something about it." The Christian points to the cross and says, "He did! He did!" '

The answer to our conundrum can be found only in the cross, for there is the biggest conundrum of all. 'God forsaken by God!' as St Anselm observed. 'How can it be?' 'The immortal dies,' sang Charles Wesley in his great hymn. The Almighty becomes vulnerable and helpless. Yet because of the cross we have the Resurrection. From the worst thing that man could do to anyone, came the greatest thing that God can do for everyone. God brought the greatest good from out of the greatest evil. Our experience, and that of many others, is that in the dark days God draws really close. My wife and I would both say that we have never experienced so deeply the love and warmth and strength of God's presence with us as when our son died. He drew near to us in an almost tangible way; he drew near through his people, who comforted us practically with meals and gifts and their boundless love. We can say from our hearts, with Paul, the words he wrote to the Christians in Corinth:

'Praise be to the God and Father of our Lord Jesus Christ, the Father of compassion and the God of all comfort, who comforts us in all our troubles, so that we can comfort those in any trouble with the comfort we ourselves have received from God. For just as the sufferings of Christ flow over into our lives, so also through Christ our comfort overflows.' (2 Corinthians 1:3-5.)

So we've established two things: God in Jesus knows all about 'bad' things — he's been there! He's experienced many of the worst things that man can do to man. Secondly, the cross and the Resurrection show that he can and does bring good out of evil, that positive things can happen as a result of tragedy and disaster. This is in no way to say that God caused the tragedy in order to bring about the good; life caused the tragedy, but God was present with those caught up in it, and used it for good.

One question remains: why didn't God intervene? Why didn't he stop the accident, avert the tragedy? Why didn't an all-knowing, all-powerful God intervene to stop the tragedy from happening? This is perhaps the hardest question of all. And at the risk of being accused of ducking it, I have to say simply, 'I don't know'. There is a mystery at the heart of life, at the heart of death, at the heart of God. So I, the creature, cannot question my Creator, or fathom his mind, as Job discovered: ' "Surely I speak of things I do not understand; things too wonderful for me to know." ' (Job

42:3.) And yet, and yet, we can't quite be satisfied with leaving it there. Our questing, questioning minds cannot fully rest content. If God never intervenes, is he no longer interested in this world today? If God never intervenes, what's the use of prayer? What is guidance for? Does he not 'direct our paths'?

I want to affirm that he does; he does break into life; he does hear and answer prayer (though not always as we want, or in the time-scale we'd like). He is a living, loving, active God, alert in the world today, alive in his people. So why does he not intervene to prevent tragedy and disaster? I believe that he does, but to our earthly eyes apparently in a random, selective way. For example, during Jesus' ministry he raised three people to life; but thousands died whom he didn't. He healed a number of men with leprosy; but a far greater number were not healed. He cured 'great multitudes' of people (Matthew 4:23-25; 15:30; 19:2); but not everyone in Israel. In other words, the ministry of Jesus – bringing healing and wholeness – was selective, apparently random. He looked for faith or trust, but it wasn't a necessary condition in every case. And he never, never said, 'If you only had more faith I could heal you', as some Christians assert.

His intervening is very real and certain, as many, many praying Christians will testify; he may not avert the tragedy, but he will be a strength and a stay to those who are caught up in it and who look to him. His intervening may appear to us to be random and selective, but it is always loving and compassionate. And so I believe it is right to pray for God to intervene – he prompts us to – to believe that he can and will and does intervene in the affairs of mankind. And if he doesn't appear to hear our prayers, it must not dent our faith in any way; his time-scale is not the same as ours, nor are his ways (Isaiah 55:8, 9).

We conclude, then: God is all-loving; God is all-powerful; He is sovereign Lord. He is concerned passionately and *com*passionately with this world, his world, his people, whom he does direct and guide. But we are also subject, at the same time, to the changes and chances of life; God does not always stop the Christian's business going bankrupt in a harsh economic climate. When an aeroplane crashes, God is not going to pluck out the Christians before it hits the ground, and leave the rest to die. But we have a God who knows what it's like to suffer injustice and indignity, terrible pain and agonising death.

We worship a God who, in Jesus, has himself experienced and suffered all the bad things that life can throw at us; who has, in Jesus, conquered death and given us the hope and promise of everlasting life.

We worship a God who comes to us in good times and in bad, and strengthens us with the comfort of his presence, and points us to his eternal kingdom, where there are no more tears, no more pain, no more suffering. We can rejoice at being citizens of the Kingdom of God, which is the true reality, where every good thing is stored up for God's people. So we can say from our hearts with Paul:

'I consider that our present sufferings are not worth comparing with the glory that will be revealed in us. . . . Who shall separate us from the love of Christ? Shall trouble or hardship or persecution or famine or nakedness or danger or sword? . . . No, in all these things we are more than conquerors through him who loved us. For I am convinced that neither death nor life, . . . nor anything else in all creation, will be able to separate us from the love of God that is in Christ Jesus our Lord.' (Romans 8:18, 35, 37-39.)

You cannot be more positive than that!

chapter

A matter of death and life

Christianity is rightly considered to be a life-and-death matter, but I would suggest that it is very much more a matter of death and life. And this is true on three levels.

First, at the heart of our faith is the fact of the death of Jesus, and his rising to new life – forever. The cross comes before the Resurrection.

It is also a matter of the death of the individual, and his or her finding new life in Christ – forever (Romans 6:8-11). We are called upon to die to self and to live for Christ (Galatians 2:20).

We have tried to show what living for Christ entails, what the new life in Christ can and should mean, how to be more effective as salt of the earth, and how to start becoming positive people in the world. In other words, if we have 'died with Christ' in the spiritual sense, what it will mean to live in him – forever (Romans 6:8). For the eternal life he offers us begins now.

But there's a third stratum of understanding that needs to be looked at when we say that Christianity is a matter of death and life. And that is in the physical sense: there is life after death.

The 'Is there life after death?' question is one many people ponder, but hardly dare to ask. Yet Christianity certainly affirms that there *is* life after death, and so we should be able to make some positive assertions about it. But these must not be mere speculation.

Shakespeare's Hamlet famously described death as 'that country from which no traveller has e'er returned'. To that the Christian can respond, 'We believe – we know – that Christ returned from that country and that, through his resurrection, we have the promise of our own eternal life.'

In Matthew's gospel the Sadducees, who did not believe in the resurrection, put a trick question to Jesus: Whose wife in the resurrection, they wanted to know, will a woman be who was married to seven different brothers in turn. ' "You are in error because you do not know the Scriptures or the power of God," ' Jesus replied (22:23-29).

What *is* this 'power of God'? Where is it most vividly shown? The answer must be in the resurrection, in raising Jesus from the dead. As Paul writes, 'By his power God raised the Lord from the dead, and he will raise us also.' (1 Corinthians 6:14.) And again, 'That power is like the working of his mighty strength, which he exerted in Christ when he raised him from the dead.' (Ephesians 1:19, 20.)

So we can conclude that our answers will be found in the Bible, and in a deeper awareness of the power of God in raising Jesus from the dead.

What happens at death is, on one level, quite simple: the body dies, ceases to function, disintegrates, perishes. Christianity has never taught that the dead human body is other than 'perishable'. 'The dust returns to the ground it came from.' (Ecclesiastes 12:7.) And yet, from the first, there was the affirmation of resurrection: 'For I know that my Redeemer liveth, and that he shall stand at the latter day upon the earth: and though after my skin worms destroy this body, yet in my flesh shall I see God.' (Job 19:25, 26, KJV.)

David Winter in his little book *Hereafter* argues that, though the post-resurrection appearance of Jesus was changed, he specifically denied that he was a ghost or spirit (Luke 24:38, 39), adding 'and clearly he was not, because he could be touched, and he was able to prepare and eat a meal'. Yet the risen Christ *was* different: he was immortal. Winter quotes Paul's claim that 'Christ being raised from the dead, will never die again; death has no longer dominion over him.' He adds, 'That in itself says something about the body of Jesus after his resurrection.

'All human bodies are mortal. They lie under the "dominion of death". Or, to put it in more usual language, they begin to die from the moment they are born. But this new body of Jesus was not subject either to the sudden onslaught of disease or accident, nor to the insidious and irresistible process of growing old.' David Winter, *Hereafter* (Hodder), page 62, *et seq.*

So the post-resurrection body of Jesus was changed, but he was still recognisably the same person. Outside the tomb, Mary of Magdala recognised him by his voice. The disciples on the road to Emmaus found their 'eyes . . . opened' so that they recognised Jesus when he asked the blessing on the food (Luke 24:30, 31). It is likely that the disciples who went fishing on Galilee recognised Jesus by his instruction to ' "Throw your net on the right side of the boat . . ." ' (John 21:6), a similar instruction to the one he had given when he had first called them from the sea to be 'fishers of men' (Mark 1:17). It was the miracle he had done, and the personality they knew so well, that made them recognise the one who had built a fire and made them breakfast.

The fifteenth chapter of Paul's first letter to the Corinthians is the great chapter on the resurrection. Paul states the essence of Christian belief this way: 'That Christ died for our sins according to the Scriptures, that he was buried, that he was raised on the third day according to the Scriptures, and that he appeared to Peter, and then to the Twelve. After that, he appeared to more than five hundred of the brothers at the same time, most of whom are still living, though some have fallen asleep. Then he appeared to James, then to all the apostles, and last of all he appeared to me also. . . .' (1 Corinthians 15:3-8.) Paul argues for the literal resurrection of Jesus in some detail continuing, 'But if it is preached that Christ has been raised from the dead, how can some of you say that there is no resurrection of the dead? If there is no resurrection of the dead, then not even Christ has been raised. And if Christ has not been raised, our preaching is useless and so is your faith. . . . If Christ has not been raised, your faith is futile; you are still in your sins. Then those also who have fallen asleep in Christ are lost. If only for this life we have hope in Christ, we are to be pitied more than all men' (verses 12-19).

Paul continued: *'But Christ has indeed been raised from the dead, the firstfruits of those who have fallen asleep. For since death came through a man, the resurrection of the dead comes also through a man. For as in Adam all die, so in Christ all will be made alive. But each in his own turn: Christ, the firstfruits; then, when he comes, those who belong to him'* (verses 20-23).

This is how Paul describes our post-resurrection bodies: 'The body that is sown is perishable, it is raised imperishable; it is sown in dishonour, it is raised in glory; it is sown in weakness, it is raised in power; it is sown a natural body, it is raised a spiritual body. . . . Listen, I tell you a mystery: We will not all sleep, but we will all be changed – in a flash, in the twinkling of an eye, at the last trumpet. For the trumpet will sound, the dead will be raised imperishable, and we will be changed. For the perishable must clothe itself with the imperishable, and the mortal with immortality. . . . "Death has been swallowed up in victory" ' (verses 42, 51-54).

What is resurrected is we ourselves, not our ghosts, not our 'souls', but our whole personality – that is what will be resurrected to live forever with God.

This passage, from which I read at my own son's funeral some years ago, is at the heart of the Christian doctrine of resurrection and immortality. Our earthly bodies die, but our recognisable personality is clothed in a new body – Jesus said 'like the angels' (Luke 20:36).

My son's body was so mauled and mangled as a result of the road accident that the funeral directors said it was 'barely recognisable' – words which stabbed my heart, for he had been a fine-looking young man. But my Christian faith, confirmed in Scripture, assures me that God will give him a new body (1 Corinthians 15:38); not 'new' in the sense of restoring the old, but a different kind of body altogether, just as Jesus' body after the resurrection was a different kind from that before. And it will be glorious! (Verse 43; Romans 8:18.) And let me dismiss the theory of reincarnation. This belief states that we return to earth in another 'live' form in a different body, perhaps as an animal or insect; the more our good deeds in our world, the higher our form of life (as insects or species of animal) when we return. Let it firmly be said that this is not a Christian view; it is nowhere in the Bible, and it is quite unworthy to be held by sincere Christians. We have a future body which is far more glorious than our human body, and no one could consider applying that marvellous word 'glorious' to an insect.

The second theory some Christians vaguely adhere to is Spiritualism. Again, there are no grounds for this in the Bible. In fact it is specifically banned in Scripture (Leviticus 20:27), and when King Saul consulted a medium and imagined that she'd summoned up the spirit of the prophet Samuel he was roundly rebuked (1 Samuel 28). Again, the tapping out of messages can hardly be described as 'glorious'.

The Christian teaching is that the resurrected body is one of splendour and beauty. Our earthbound bodies are subject to space and time, and all the physical limitations: pain and suffering, failing faculties of sight and hearing, physical handicaps, wearing out and running down.

But in the life beyond death these things don't even exist. In the penultimate chapter of the Bible John writes, 'I heard a loud voice from the throne [of heaven] saying, "Now the dwelling of God is with men, and he will live with them. They will be his people and God himself will be with them and be their God. He will wipe away every tear from their eyes. There will be no more death or mourning or crying or pain, for the old order of things has passed away." ' (Revelation 21:3, 4.)

The Christian has a great and glorious hope to look forward to. Our future life in Christ is promised, guaranteed, secure. Those in whom the Spirit of Christ now lives can look forward to a glorious future, where our personality exists in a recognisable form, but without the earthbound constraints of our physical body, our outer shell. God will give us a different kind of body, no longer 'perishable' but 'imperishable' (1 Corinthians 15:38, 42-44, 50), and it will be like the difference between a seed and the beautiful flower that springs from that seed.

Moreover, we will be dwelling with God, and he is

absolute Beauty, absolute Love. It will be Heaven – Paradise (literally) – with Christ at the centre of a community of his people, a community of *absolute* love where he dwells in the midst, where there is no more pain or sorrow, no more disease or disintegration, no more suffering or death. This is no flight of fancy. It is what the Scripture tells us, and it is the result of the Power of God in raising Jesus from the dead.

For now, we are living on earth with just one foot in heaven. Yet here and now we have this glorious eternal life, that deep spiritual life of Christ at the core of our being. With him at the centre of our lives we can and should be positive people, ever praising, ever rejoicing, for our Lord assures us we are the salt of the earth.

RESPONSE

As a positive response to God's positive action in sending **JESUS** to live for me and to die for me, I make the following vow:

I commit myself to live each day as a disciple of Jesus Christ, guided by the Holy Spirit to the glory of God the Father. So I promise to:

Pray daily
Read the Bible regularly
Attend public worship faithfully
Commend the Christian Faith by word and deed
Fashion my life according to the example of Christ
Give and forgive as generously as God has given
and forgiven me

Glorious and blessed God, Father, Son, and Holy Spirit,
May this vow now made on earth be ratified in Heaven.
Amen